Hi! I'm your new Manager!

You're new - they're not!
So what happens now?

by
Ray Labadie

authorHOUSE®

AuthorHouse™
1663 Liberty Drive, Suite 200
Bloomington, IN 47403
www.authorhouse.com
Phone: 1-800-839-8640

This book is a work of non-fiction. Unless otherwise noted, the author
and the publisher make no explicit guarantees as to the accuracy of
the information contained in this book and in some cases, names of
people and places have been altered to protect their privacy.

First published by AuthorHouse 12/31/2007

ISBN: 978-1-4343-3059-8 (sc)

Library of Congress Control Number: 2007907476

Printed in the United States of America
Bloomington, Indiana

This book is printed on acid-free paper.

Author picture, on cover, by Images Photography, Inc, of Wilson, North Carolina.

Table of Contents

Acknowledgements

Seldom is anyone successful at what they plan to do if they do not have someone to lean on, and depend on, for inspiration. I have my family. Huge thanks to my wife Nancy. Without her, I would still be a junior machine operator making six thousand dollars a year. Her silent support was always there for me and for that I will be eternally grateful. And special thanks to my sons Al and Ken. When both of them dropped out of college, I panicked and challenged them that I would get my degree before either of them. I didn't complete my degree before them but I did I get my degree and I got both of my boys to go back to college.

And a much-appreciated thank you to my friends and work associates who constantly bugged me to put my experiences on paper and get it published - in particular, Karen – many thanks for believing in me. The rest of you are too numerous to list or I'd have to release a second volume with just names. All characters and no plot makes very boring reading. I think it's called a telephone directory. Anyway, you know who you are and how much you mean to me.

My intention is not to profess expert knowledge of the management profession, but rather to convey a message that each person reading this book needs to understand - that good management is a commitment to his or her staff. Good management is seldom viewed as a successful part of a team, whereas in fact it is usually the glue that holds the team together. It is the vehicle for problem resolution, the platform for strategic growth and the reinforcement behind every successful individual. Very much like a teacher (but excluding all the parental and school board pressure), the manager must provide all the tools that make a smart individual an asset to the organization and a successor to the manager role.

I truly hope that each of you completes reading this book and thinks immediately of your favorite boss and realizes that there are parts of you which emulate him or her. Then I hope you begin the process, if you have not already done so, of preparing yourself for a long and rewarding career as a manager with a heart and soul. One who does so for the reward of watching someone elevate even higher than you and does so partially because you were there for him or her.

I dedicate this book to my mother, Rose Ann. She was my source of inspiration most of my young adult life and my very first love. I will carry her words of encouragement in my heart for as long as I live. Thanks Mom – your son, *Raymond*.

Introduction

So you are a brand new manager are you? Congratulations! This has to be exciting for you and should be a glowing moment in your career. It represents the point in your resume where you leave technical specifics and begin developing you management foundation. Here is where you begin using terms like "team building", "strategic" and "reorganized". And, as you progress, you see that your skill in a specific field is not as valuable as your ability to motivate and monitor. You can see the role that you want to evolve into but the most difficult part is knowing how to get there and what you have to do to elevate yourself in the eyes of your staff, your management and your peers.

Welcome to **Management.**

The intention of this text is to provide you with the reference information to allow you move into the next step of management – credibility. In order to make an impact on what you have been challenged with as a new manager, you need to understand …

- The company
- Your manager
- Your executive
- Your staff

- Your job
- Your goals and objectives
- The company goals and objectives
- What you should do
- What you should not do
- Where you fit into all of this
- What to look for so you can assume your new role effectively
- More, and more, and more!

That's about it! A tall order for anyone and even larger one for a person who is not yet trained on how to approach their new role and assume the responsibility of a team of people.

Here's what happened to me ...... and I'm not kidding!

When I was promoted to my first management position, I had no previous training and no idea what to expect. At the time, there were very few sources of management training and I was soon going to find out that education by osmosis was not a valid alternative. But education has two arms. The first is the classroom based education that focuses on one area and you learn how a good manager should interact with people of varying culture, age, sex and so on. You are actually taught to handle situations a specific way and why you should (or should not) use certain language – verbal or body – when interacting with one or all of your staff.

The other arm of education is the "school of hard knocks". These are the personal lessons you learn when you are being yourself. You know, when you raise your voice, or threaten someone with termination. Or, a classic example is when you ignore sage advice because the author is a "junior". Or when you attempt to elevate yourself above those who make you look good. And, of course, there is so much more but I believe you get the point. You make your greatest mistakes when you are busy being yourself. Change is what allows you to become a better person – *a better manager*.

In order to learn from either school, you have to be cognizant that something has to be learned. If you walk into either scenario with your brain off – you cannot possibly acquire new knowledge. So there has to be awareness that you are not the smartest person in the world and no one is going to name their first born after you just because you have a title of "manager". Therefore, it's time for you to see what you are doing to and with your staff. Let's start with what happened to me many years ago.

100 Years Ago ...

My first position as manager saw me staring at a job description as well as a statement that I had to fire one of my staff. Not just anyone. He was my best friend. Granted, he had performance issues but nothing was documented. I refused and risked losing my new position the same day I got it. However, I based it on what I would expect from any company – a written warning overseen by Human Resources. My boss accepted that, my best friend accepted it and HR accepted it – and life went on. But I have to tell you; it was absolute hell for the first few weeks. An invisible force was judging me and I felt helpless.

Then and there, I knew that this management role had far more impact on my life than anything else I had been asked to do. But don't get me wrong; I also knew that I was nowhere near where I needed to be in order to support my small staff. But I had no idea where to start. So I did as so many before me did – *I played it by ear.*

One thing that I had not realized was that the people I now had reporting to me – were formerly my peers. The same people I played baseball and hockey with and the same people I went out partying with on weekends, were now my staff. So now what? What am I supposed to be in their eyes? I soon found out that I only needed to be what I apparently was before the promotion. I needed to be someone they could trust, respect and enjoy working with - every day. Exactly the same way I was before I became their boss.

OK, so now I'm supposedly a reasonably good person to work with – so why do I feel I needed far more than what I was equipped with? Because, I needed to get myself educated and organized for the part of the job I never expected – **clairvoyance!** I needed to know when they were tired, how they were doing on their projects, which one was the best to lead or follow and what education they needed in order to remain challenged. Or, at least I thought I had to be that way, until I found out that proper planning <u>with</u> the employee led you to far better results and a much more satisfied staff. What a novel idea! Now I could allocate a specific amount of time every week to review and evaluate where we were relative to where we needed to be. And they were there to help me with the detail information they thrived on while I assisted with tools and education to keep them ahead of the learning curve.

The bottom line here is that my education (or lack of it) came at a cost – to the employee – whereas it should have come as a cost in monetary terms, to the company. I should have been evaluated and pointed to specific training that would benefit me, as a manager, and my staff. Without it, the employee was the recipient of my void and not my focused education. To begin with, let's look at a segment of historical evolution and see if we (or you) can learn anything from what was experienced several years ago.

And then there were Computers ...

I have been fortunate enough to work in Information Technology (IT) for over many years and have watched the IT world turn upside down nearly every decade. And now, in the twenty-first century, it's happening every 2-3 years. And it is doing so with amazing new technology like wireless (cell and blue tooth) communications, VoIP (Voice over IP) and Internet based video and voice conferencing. Megabytes have given way to terabytes and soon petabytes. MIPS are now in the tens of thousands rather than units. It is also affected by cost containment like off shore outsourced programming and development. There have been several consecutive upheavals in the world of IT. I've witnessed and experienced most of them, and the management that came along with it. But not all of it has been good for the employee.

Commercial IT began with massive computing engines processing millions of punched cards with readers, cardpunch units and printers. It was called Data Processing. The processors were single step initiated machines in that they could perform only one processing function at a time. Because of that, a single program owned the machine along with all peripherals. Kind of like your mother owning your mind and entire nervous system while she pinched your ear between her thumb and forefinger. I bet you never did that again.

Anyway, programming was contained to only those few engineers who had access to the reference manuals and the hardware. This is when I came into the world of DP. The staff was just evolving from the IBM 1401 to the IBM 360 (I know, I told you I was old) with thousands of instructions per minute, 64K of memory and printers that would set you on your butt if you touched them before grounding yourself. They were self centered and extremely possessive - and so were the engineers.

Managers were just learning the ropes. They had to work with people who had no computer experience and make them aware of the potential loss incurred by a simple programming or execution mistake. The horror of "Job Reruns" and the need to verify and re-verify changes were constantly part of the conversation. There were no manuals and even fewer management rules to live by.

Change ....

A couple years later, a new technology came along – magnetic media that allowed you to actually store your data on a reel of tape. It was nothing more than a high-speed reel-to-reel recording device. The emergence of magnetic tape drives gave us a means of recording data and playing it back the same way it was recorded. Data archives meant we could now manage a master file of data without having to re-punch cards to carry the previous and the present bank account balances, meter readings, invoices and so much more. We thought that was exciting until a few years after that, magnetic disk drives were born. Cool! Now we could create a master file, delete it and re-create it using control commands from the master console or using this new thing called "Job Control Language" – or JCL. If that wasn't enough to make programmers cough up their coding pencils, the mainframe evolved into multi-processing.

This was too much. Now, a programmer no longer had full ownership of the processor when he/she coded their works of art – they had to share memory and peripherals. It was here that I saw the first migration of programmers running away from computers and into more stable areas like Finance and Production Control. So did the managers. The older staff could no longer accept owning only a portion of the machines while something else was assuming another portion of the processor activity. They definitely were not into sharing.

Management was still about the same. Planning was focused around design and development – but not the development of the employee. That seemed to be a known responsibility of the manager but he or she had little available to them other than a job description to reference when considering training & education. Training was focused on technology and not on how to be a better manager. Even more emphasis was placed on HR to support the rest of the business community.

While technology was elevating, so was the person working with that technology. Then, along came the freshly trained college students who were more than willing to take on this new development environment. And they were good at it too. They were young, cocky and full of energy and enthusiasm to learn and grow. The intimidated old-timers gradually pulled out and retired or transferred. It was far easier to leave the environment than admit to obsolescence. Management had a new opportunity – to keep very sharp people challenged and rewarded when they accomplish what they have been assigned.

More Change

Then telecommunications was born. This really exciting world of entering something into a dumb terminal in one building and having the mainframe (in yet another building or country) actually respond with information and the verification of what you just entered – in seconds. It was all handled through a slow speed telephone line (or hard wiring like coaxial cabling) back to the mainframe. More programmers dropped their keyboards and ran for higher ground because of this crazy world of pseudo-conversational and quasi-reentrant coding. Imagine, someone could actually blow your program away while it was executing – and it wasn't the operator (whom everything was usually blamed on). Now they had to share everything. There were very few that stayed the course in IT. More were leaving IT for finance and the plant floor and high school/college graduates were quickly taking their place. These fresh students were not intimidated by the speed of evolution or the new tools that were coming out every day. Yet this was a wonderful opportunity for management to take these perfect pieces of putty and mould them into fine management machines. Succession planning wasn't in the air yet. Instead, they chose "fast track" where these bright, young people were exposed to the company and quickly elevated to senior positions – without management training. Once again, the employee loses.

Even more change ...

Soon afterwards came the world of LAN/WAN and the PC. It was amazing how many people thought that the PC was a fad that would fade away in 4-5 years. Obviously they were unquestionably wrong. But now a program could be developed that didn't even run on a mainframe. And, the mainframe didn't know it existed. Older programmers were taking medication just to get up on the morning. Alienation was the "feeling du jour".

Teenagers were now overtaking the brave new world of computing - many of them, while they were still going to public school. This exciting world of technology was wide open for new development that the mainframe software vendors had not even thought to exploit. Does the name Bill Gates mean anything to you?

Work term students were born in the 70's and 80's and because of that a student could graduate with 2-3 years of experience. No longer was a degree the only item in their hand. I personally loved the students as they brought something into the organization other than reducing the mean average of age. They brought *fresh new thinking*. They were the ones who asked "Why".

Most of the established full time employees were sitting on their suppositories when these bright-eyed learners were making suggestions based on keen observations. These ideas broke away from the traditional thinking that had historically been foregone conclusions. Unfortunately, elevated costs brought organizational changes whereby Human Relations or Employee Relations decided that the manager should carry more of this responsibility so it was moved into the manager role – without training & education.

Now, in the twenty-first century, managers are expected to dig deeper into problems and own them. This, of course, means that they needed to be trained on how to complete numerous forms that were historically managed by HR. Managers are also expected to handle tense situations and know when to bring HR into the picture. While researching problems and invoking new procedures to correct them, I began to run across "the attitude".

Because of that, I began taking notes on how to motivate people and found that, in order to be successful, I first had to win their trust. That is never easy but the majority of people are looking for good, reliable leadership and once they believe they have that, they will do what ever it takes to do the job the way it should be done. It is that small minority of people – those who are always looking for ways to avoid work, responsibility and accountability – who need to understand that they need to change or go home.

OK – back to the topic at hand.

Today

So here we are today with a telephone/PDA strapped to our waste and staying in touch with the entire organization while we are on vacation. There is no such thing as an eight-hour day and the demands and pressures of the working world are greater than ever – especially for "The New Manager". So what have you done before taking on this hugely burdened position? Saying the rosary, lighting candles or aromatherapy are excellent for mental and spiritual relaxation – but the real answers are in the way you are educated and how well you relate to your staff.

The point behind all this babble is that 40 years ago, a problem could occur, get caught during the output phase and it could be fixed in the next day or two – and the customer did not suffer. Actually, they never knew because the delay from transactional preparation to production final run took days. Recovery was as slow as the normal processing so no one was usually any the wiser if a programming mistake or operator error, forced a rerun. Back then, a computer, or anything related to it, was in the realm of rocket science and only the "brainy" people worked in that role. Not any more! This computer thing is now in the hands of children and every year it is getting closer to being in the hands of infants. The real key was that business was based on an 8 hour day – that gave us 16 additional hours to fix our mistakes, plus weekends.

Not any more ....

Today, daily processing is totally different. Think of the banking field where bank branches close at 5:00 PM or 6:00 PM (in many cases these days branches are in grocery stores and close at 8:00 or 9:00 PM). Item Processing (checks and the like) are gathered and processed in preparation for a nightly production run. Production processing begins to apply postings of debits and credits from various sources so that the files can be up by 8:00 AM the next morning. That means that you have 8 hours to do all your backups in preparation for the morning production processing and then clear all of your files and storage areas for the next days lightning speed processing.

Wait a minute – what about Central, Mountain and Pacific Time zones. If the same mainframe, or processor, performs all the work, you have to wait until all of the files are unlocked for all accounts (unless you have a sophisticated environment that allows you to freeze and process accounts in one time zone while the other active time zones can continue). You just lost three more hours. You are now down to 5 hours. And what about having the possibility of a rerun? You have to allow for that or you are digging yourself an early grave. Now you are down to two and one half hours for every form of processing before the data files need to be up and accessible. Pray to your God that early retirement is available for you if the master files are not available for the general public by 8:00 AM.

OOPS – forgot about the web world. People traveling to Europe who want to pay their bills need access where their day is our night. So what are you going to do for them?

Get my point?

Forty years ago, management was a slightly different art than today. There was pressure, but not near as much as today. There were time constraints, but not like the ones we live with every day. And there were people who needed training, but not near the volume of T&E needed to keep pace with the demands of today. And it was a chauvinistic world that ignored the perceived peons and sexual intimidation was rampant. Thank goodness legislation and evolution have allowed us to be treated as human beings and we can gain the respect of an informed executive just by doing our job *that you are busy building your career and ignoring their needs. These types of managers make decisions that alienate them from the teams and prevent the customer from getting what they need – the highest possible service level from your team at the lowest possible cost. Now, is that last statement an oxymoron or can it actually be achieved. The answers are No and Yes, respectively.*

Excellent management training can make you a superb manager but will not provide you with awareness of the "business". Too much business training can make you a shining star to the executives and alienate you from your staff. As in all cases, the key to success is when you know what to do and what to expect so you can prepare for it and execute when the time is required.

As a new manager or a person armed with executive or corporate goals and objectives that show aspirations of management, the first thing you need to understand is that in order to manage people properly you have to be fearless and passionate. Being fearless, means that you can approach your staff one at a time, or in groups, to address tough issues. This must be done with the intention of seeing the elimination of each issue while having the best interests of the people and the company, in mind. The passion is the self-confidence you exude as you lead your team through the plethora of problems that you have to resolve every day. This also includes the advice you give to them when they come to you with business or personal problems.

The greatest key to success is having respect for yourself and your team. Treat them the way you want to be treated with consistency and without compromise. Remember, chances are very good that your job could be eliminated tomorrow and their job will remain because they have the technical knowledge and you probably don't. So now that you are viewed as a waste of time (because you are new to your job) how do you go about changing that so the respect can be both ways? It's easy! You can do it in small and manageable steps so that you grow with your team. The speed is entirely up to you (or the objectives given you by your executive) but too slow is endless and too fast will encourage failure. You have to feel the speed of change. Sometimes it comes from an executive warning that they will not accept a project being late. Sometimes it's from a competitor's announcement of a product you don't have. Both imply that you have to complete it yesterday. And both suggest that your only alternative to success is sliding down a banister made of razor blades. One takes a lot more effort than the other and the results are a lot less painful.

First you need to know yourself and your limitations. Then you need to find out the same of each person who reports to you. Start with the basics (that is about all I am qualified to offer anyway) and let the ideas start to flow in all directions. I guarantee you that unless you have inherited an unruly street gang; they are just looking for fair and firm leadership – just what you are capable of providing.

And it has to be fun!!!

If you can't have some fun, as far as I am concerned, it's not worth doing. Now, granted, there are jobs out there which demand sobriety and total focus. I certainly wouldn't want an air traffic controller attempting to crack jokes with the flight crew while an emergency landing was taking place – especially if I am one of the passengers. But there is always a time and a place to relax and enjoy the company of your team.

I have numbered the chapters but that is only because a book with one chapter isn't going to encourage anyone to read it. A thousand plus pages is a competitor to War and Peace as well as a proven sleep aid. So I have created this short document as a foundation for learning and from here you can direct yourself to those who have made it their life to educate you on interpersonal skills, project management methodologies and personal growth references. I am merely giving you my personal experiences and references so you can weigh them and determine what, if not all, of my findings will assist you in being a better person and a stronger manager.

Now, have fun reading this book and then put it to work! I assure you, most of your staff will appreciate it. The ones that don't may well be fodder for your next reorganization requirements.

Chapter One – Org Charts, Titles and Responsibilities.

"Getting organized doesn't mean you know what you are doing. It just means you're doing it better than you were before you got organized".

I have been fortunate enough to have changed jobs several times from promotions. And I have seen more job changes because companies I have worked for have this uncanny habit of being sold or closing less than two years after I join them. In each case I had to start from square one in learning my new management, the teams I would be managing, the peers I would be working with and the expectations of all the above. I love it. There is nothing better than taking on a problem. My greatest concern has always been to assume the helm of a perfect team and not having anything to do – except potentially messing it all up.

So which one are you? I sure hope you aren't the one inheriting a strong team because, unless your manager properly groomed you and explained what he or she did to get it to that point, you may well have the curse of the red felt tipped pen on you. You know! The pen you put in your pocket or case but failed to place the top on the end so now you have that huge stain for all to see. You always feel so special at times like that.

So what are the first steps in getting your act together? You are indeed in luck as I have my personal list of "To Do" items that I will share with you so that you can walk into any role and assume control. Except at home – that's between you and your partner as I am a lousy match maker, a so-so husband and certainly not a person to be referenced for sage partner advice.

First step – get information!

Unless you could care less (in which case I'd suggest you find a new career) your first step should be to learn as much as you can about your staff and then meet them so you can match everything you have gathered to what they believe. So to begin the fact-finding mission, get an organization chart of your team(s) and learn how you are currently organized. Get some history on the team from your boss and your peers but don't pass judgment even after you have had a chance to see how your team operates. Keep in mind that they have never worked for you before so they – and you – have something to learn about each other. But you definitely have to learn and understand what their priorities are (your interviews of them) compared to what they should be (feedback from your management). If they are already in alignment – great – sit back and count your blessings.

Even if you are assuming the management of a team you were previously part of, I suggest you learn your team organization and see what your manager has to say about it. It is amazing what goes on in the department that the manager never complains about – and at some point you may have been one of those issues. Remember, chances are slim that what you hear is what you expect. Take special note in what you don't hear (like the lack of praises of and for each other) and keep them in mind as you go about determining where your focus should be in your first few weeks.

Organization

Is your team organized for success or failure? Talk with your manager to see why they are aligned the way they are today and see if you have any elbow room to make changes. It is absolutely imperative that you and your team both conform to any change (if required). If they already accept you as their manager, you are a leg up on your transition so that means you can concentrate on productivity and efficiency.

So what can an organization chart tell you? How about who has the most responsibility in your team? Let's look at the chart below and see if the load is unbalanced.

What do you see here? Debbie has the most people so she must have the most difficult job. Just a minute, Habib does all the script work for your team as well as for two of your peers, so he must have the most difficult job. Hold on, I hear that Bob does all the architectural design for the company – so he must have the most difficult job since there are six development and script teams.

There's only one way to find out – talk with them after to list your questions. Ask them with the intention of finding out how they are working and not as an inquisition. If you want to gain ground, interact as their ally and mentor and not as if they are doing something wrong and you're going to fix it.

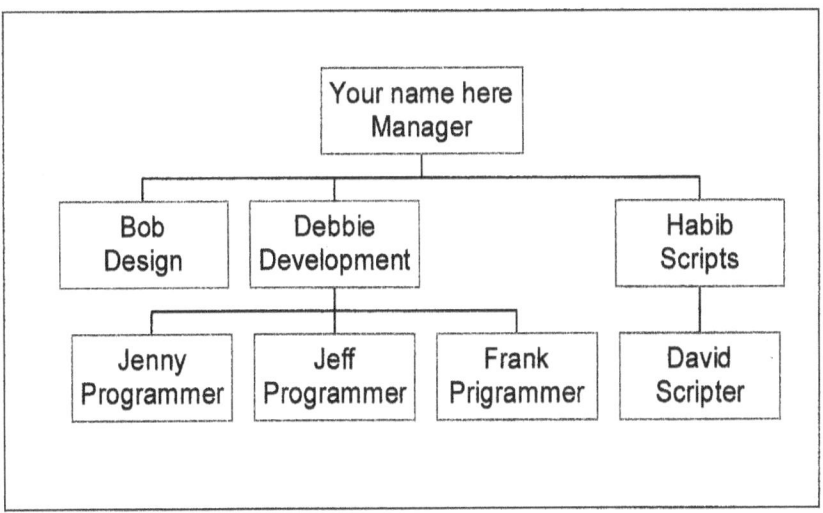

Keep in mind that your intention is to determine where they are at as a team as well as at the individual level. What you are acquiring here is information for future reference:

- Potential for elevation to more responsibility and supervisory/management training.
- Personal development - is there an immediate need for technical education?
- Team player – do they mix and match?
- Interpersonal skills – how well do they interact with you, the others, management, customers?
- Subject expertise – how well do they know their product and how they are supporting it?
- Work level – are they over their heads or just snowed under with work?
- Who they are – it is just as important to know who they are and what they value outside the job, as it is to know if they are contributing to the work effort.
- What do they think of the team, their productivity, the department, the company, their jobs, the products, the way they work, the environment?

At no point should there be a need for you to scowl – unless you suddenly realized you only put deodorant under one armpit. Maintain a studious look and don't forget to smile – it actually looks good on you and it certainly puts the tension at a lower level.

If you have a charter that has been assigned to you, it should also come out at this time. You will be amazed how much the people appreciate being part of the big picture instead of scratching at the frosted surface to see what is underneath.

The best part of this process is finding out what these people want to be – in the next 1-3 years. However, you need to be prepared for those who are happier than a duck in water to be in their job and want to remain in it until Gabriel or retirement calls. There is nothing wrong with being a professional "X" forever. Unless that is, the need for that function is eliminated with progressive changes. But that is your job too. You need to make sure that the people are constantly attempting to elevate themselves even if it does not mean a promotion. The demand for faster and better is based on increased productivity. Antiquation is a result of poor planning and the person in that role is not at fault. You need to look after the people who are looking after you. It's called a partner handshake. Many people handle it different ways. It depends on the work environment, the company position on relationship management and the need for you and your staff to be close and relating to one another every day. I can see where the military cannot allow that to happen. If you get too close, it could cost you and your team, their lives. High-pressure positions usually cannot allow a "buddy" relationship. If you give too much leniency to anyone, it could come back to haunt you.

Assuming you have an office environment that builds close teams, then work with that and see if it is something that is good for you and your team. If, after a short period of time you cannot see it working then you need to re-evaluate the posture. You may have to make changes where you can reach the desired goals based on the relationship needed to get the job done.

Job Descriptions

The job descriptions are usually the tell-all of what is happening and how well the person is relating to their job. In many cases, organizations like to have a reasonably well defined job description with the stand by statement of "other duties when required" so the people can work in varying capacities. This allows the company to deviate the roles so they do not need to re-write the job role every year as it evolves over time. As the company grows or various conditions demand more precision in the job role it is probably best for the people and the company that it stay that way. However, the meat of the job still has to be in the role.

Speaking of working to the true definition of the role, I can recall walking by the desk of our AA shortly after starting my new job as the Director of IT with a marketing firm and I saw her entering data into an Excel spreadsheet. It was statistics on the production from each of our call centers across the states. That was not unusual, except that the source of her entry was a stack of faxes of yet another spreadsheet. Needless to say, I stopped and asked her how much of her time was spent doing that activity (thinking this was a classic case of time saving through automation) and she stated that it took her almost four hours every day. So I searched for specifics and merely asked what it was she was actually doing – in a kind voice of course. Her response was that she was consolidating the call center statistics into one spreadsheet from the six call centers and then forwarding the summary document to our corporate office in New York. I then asked her if she ever asked why the information was not automatically consolidated using an electronic file transfer process and Excel spreadsheet merges and I got this response:

"This is the way I was trained to do it and I've been doing it this way for four years."

Well, if you know me you'd also know that the small hairs on the nap of my neck stand up straight when I hear one of my five favorite phrases – and that was one of them. I asked her what she did after she completed the entry and I was advised she e-mailed it to the head of our Finance department in New York.

I went back to my office and called that Finance person and she confirmed that she receives this file from my AA every day and has done so for the last four years. Before I could ask my next question she quickly added: **"And I don't know why because we started receiving them from the branches directly almost two years ago".** I then asked what she did with the document from our AA and she stated that she deleted the file. I nearly spit out my teeth – and they aren't false.

As you might expect, I went back to our AA and filled her in on what was happening and that she no longer needed to receive those sheets and that they were being sent to New York. Her next response was that it was great because she has been working overtime for the last four years trying to get everything done in one day. I confirmed this with our HR summary documents and we reduced our department costs that same day. We also began a weekly update of process changes that was distributed to everyone in the department so they viewed all future changes and they too could plan their day.

The job description is the heart of everyone's reason for being in that company and doing that specific job. If the world that job occupant lives in changes, the role needs to reflect it. I have seen where people were working in jobs with descriptions that were more than five years old and when reading through them, I realized that the person was working in functions that were nowhere near the description. One of two things needs to happen and both are a result of doing a performance review with the job description in front of you and the employee. Either the job is antiquated and needs to be eliminated or the job description needs to be updated. Because of these changes, the job may be elevated and the person may be eligible for a salary increase. However, beware the ill-informed. Unless you are very careful in the way you apply the changes and validate risk and associated demands, you could very well end up with an evaluation that yields a job grade below what it was. Now wouldn't that be sweet? How do you face the person who has been down graded and tell them that their grade 7 job is now graded a 6? Bring plenty of bandages and pain killer medication. You are going to need it.

It is your responsibility to assure that everyone working with you has an accurate and updated job description. The basics of the job needs to be in printed format, expressed in a way that there is no question what the person was hired to do and filed in a common reference area so it can be retrieved and reviewed annually.

A Little History

Assuming you now have a file on each person that you will maintain for any future reference, you need to look for past issues too. Has this person ever had a need for disciplinary measures? Who was the manager at the time and what has happened to him or her. It's always interesting to see where someone has been reprimanded for something and the person who managed him or her was released or demoted. Too often a person must live through the period of having a weak or intimidating manager and their file never gets updated. Make sure there are no open holes in your files. If there are, follow up and clear up any pending issues so you have people reporting to you who know you want them there and you care about their happiness in their job.

What about awards? Have your people received any in the form of commendations, a bonus, a gift or a promotion? Look through their files. If you find out later that they achieved a level of accomplishment that should have been rewarded – go to the well and see what you can do for them. Naturally, if it's not in their file you will probably find out during your staff interviews. But be sure to make notes and follow up.

You now have files, organization charts and job descriptions for your staff. What about the rest of the company? Do you know how your manager's boss is organized? If not, you need to, and here's why – what if you are asked to fill in for him or her for a few hours, a few days, a week or forever? Having a solid understanding of where your boss fits into the organization provides you with food for growth. You will undoubtedly meet and work with his peers thus knowing their responsibility is just as important as knowing yours. You will have questions that need to be asked so why not ask the right person and save yourself some embarrassment and lost time? Get to know them and the peers of your manager. Depending on your job, you may well have to provide a support service to them (like those in Information Technology). How you relate to them and perform your tasks can determine your long term relationship with them. They can be your best ally or worst enemy.

HR – Your link to everything!

Take a look at the other departments in the company. Since you now have responsibility for staff, you need to become more than casually familiar with Human Resources (HR) and Finance. HR can be one of your very best allies too. They provide you with flexibility that is not inside your budget. They can introduce you to a contractor program when your demands are high but you cannot increase head count. They can provide you with student services or work term students at a lower rate than hiring a contractor, if you are trying to build (or re-build) your team. Sometimes they can arrange for it to happen over a summer and assume all the cost while you get all the benefit of having additional help to get you over the hump of a large project.

Finance

Finance is another great ally. They can keep you abreast of where you are on your capital and expense spending. They can let you know when your depreciation schedule is going to go down and can hold capital costs over a fiscal year if you work closely with them at year end. Give them enough lead-time and they can let you know where you are on assets and whether you are being accidentally hit with depreciation that is not even yours. They can help you determine a depreciation schedule on an acquisition and whether it should be amortized over 2, 3 or 5 years – or more. Any of these can reduce your budget and make you look like a hero to your boss.

Facilities

And don't forget Facilities. These down trodden people are the very backbone of the organization and get the least credit for what they do for you. They are the ones who upgrade your furniture to assure it meets the ergonomic demands of the workplace. They provide desks, filing cabinets, fax machines and photocopiers. They build the cubicles and then tear them down and move them when you realize that you needed two more people than you thought. All of this is done without ever walking behind you and slapping the back of your head with an open palm. They can be your "OOPS" factor in that they can make up for the things you forgot to do. They coordinate the electricians, plumbers, city inspectors and contractors. They worry about asbestos while you only concern yourself with how to spell it. Most of all, they manage the floor space costs and work with all the vendors to make certain the company gets a fair shake for the dollar spent. While they are managing the number of parking spots available, you can put together proposal floor plans of where your extra filing cabinet will fit. It's a heck of a job they perform and, like the silent heroes of any company; they seldom get the proper recognition for what they do.

Information Technology

Oh yes, then there is the body of people least understood and most often cursed for what they do to us - Information Technology. They too can be an unbelievable asset. Yes, they can also be a liability when your PC breaks and they respond in three days or when your circuit to an Internet Service Provider (ISP) chokes and your Dunn and Bradstreet report is a day late getting back to you — but the pros very much outweigh the cons.

For example, when the plague of viruses hit in 2003, were you reading the paper and finding out about it or were you one of those first hand experience people? Did you go through the day as unaware of the issue as a pastor on a fishing trip in the mountains or were you sitting at your desk starring at a dead screen? Keep in mind that IT has a huge responsibility in the form of providing you with clean, reliable software running on current hardware and connecting to redundant, secure network links. They have enough problems without having to look out for employees who insist on searching XXX web sites and picking up viruses while loading a screen saver from MAD magazine.

IT can provide you with software that, within reason, meets your needs and runs reliably on compatible hardware today and tomorrow. They can provide you with unlimited storage of your files and paper products. They can guarantee backup and recovery of your most important files and provide you with emergency recovery facilities if you experience an impact to your business area. And that is where the robber meets the rogue.

Too often IT personnel are perceived as people who are constantly increasing the cost of service and the business unit is guilty of not seeing the need for firewalls and virus protection until it is too late. From my 40 years in IT, I have seen every department speak poorly of IT until the time came to fall back on them in the form of an emergency. So my suggestion is to relate to IT (no special privileges) and treat them as a business ally and you will have a rewarding career.

Like facilities, IT can also offset human error. For example, how often does someone remember that when you move your office to the other side of the city that your phone number may have to change? They know that so that you don't have to.

I'm not saying to ignore Sales, Marketing, Engineering, Product Development, Operations or any of the other departments. However, I am saying that there are versatile utility people out there who can make your life very pleasant or as miserable as a bar tender in a dry county.

Your Job

You've done a fine job of looking after your staff, but what about you? You need to verify that your job description does not conflict with those of your staff. Yet, you have to make sure there is overlap. Many of my past direct reports will look at the following picture and say **"Oh yes Ray's favorite picture"**. But it is exactly how I feel you should be managing. Take at look at the diagram on the next page. That is how I have seen most organizations that I have managed before I arrived.

Team? – Not Really!

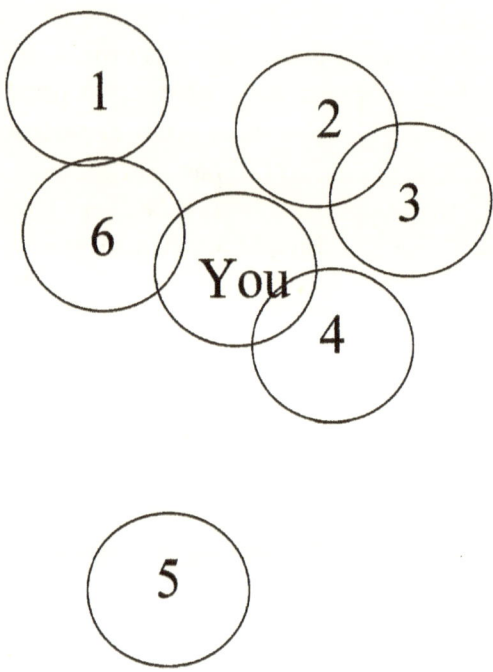

This is how the team was relating. The manager was very close to one employee, two were relatively close to the manager, two others were close to each other but not to the manager and one person was outright removed. Not good. This team was dysfunctional and in no way could they properly communicate with each other let alone me, their manager, or with the client. It had to change and it had to happen quickly.

So what would you do? Well, like any other plan you have to start with an objective. My objective was to create a team that looked more like the following diagram. What are the differences? There are many so let's cover them one at a time.

Chapter Two: Make a list of key information:

"Once you get a plan – stick to it – it's probably the only one you will have".

Unless you have been trained for the job, chances are that you will require a great deal of information so that you can fit in, be effective and be efficient. Start with a request for information that you can use to begin your evaluation of your team. Get data that will allow you to get closer to them in understanding who they are and what you should expect of them in the next 90 days. You need information about what they do, how they do it, how successful they are and when, if ever, they have failed. How happy or upset are they? What are their goals – individually or as a team.

Before you flip this page, try to determine what the list would look like. Write them down and then compare your list to mine. Take your mind out of the "I have no idea" gear and just think about what their day consists of, the pressures they have and the demands of the customers or customer support areas they manage. Do what you always do to seek out information. Start with what makes a person tick, the incidentals of their job and of course, the fact they are human and have needs.

They have rituals that you need to know about and understand (superstitions too). They have constraints in many areas and freedom in others. Your focus should be around their constraints for now. You should be working with them to release them from anything that prevents them from doing their job in an environment of maximum efficiency. Then review the freedoms – it may be that what they think they have authorization for is in fact a violation of company policy – like using the department fax for personal activities. You need to find out more about their work environment too. How clean is it? How healthy is it? How humane is it? What is it they are supposed to be doing? What is it that they are actually doing? What about performance - their performance and that of the overall department?

And how are they managing their work? Do they follow standards & procedures or are they "winging it"? Do they document their work? Do they have processes that make them efficient or are they victims of "this is the way we have always done it"?

Can you trust them?

Who's the smartest, the fastest, the hardest working? And has anyone ever thought about succession planning? If so, why wasn't one of them chosen instead of you? Who has the most education and who has the least? Who is there all the time and who is always late arriving and early to leave? Who are the most respected and why is he or she being viewed that way? Who is the best under pressure? Who is the worst? Who is the most likely to succeed you – with a little effort – or a lot?

What is your department rapport like in the business community? Do your customers like what your team does? Does your team get a lot of awards or none at all? Where does your team's output compare to the rest of the North American working world? Why?

How much money is spent on training & education each year? Who gets it and who doesn't? What type of educational spend does your company support – if at all? Is there a reimbursement plan for extended personal education? If so, who on your team has initiated an agreement with the company to get their degree, a Masters, a Doctorate?

Of all the questions on your mind, what is the most critical to you and your team? And what are you going to ask for to get the answers you need?

Start with the basics ....

1. An organization chart of your team showing your position and the person to whom you report. You need to get an executive organization chart of your company showing the main departments. By doing that, you'll know who your customer is (if you are new to the company or the area you are going to manage). Acquire a copy of your manager's organization chart as well. So you can see the names and titles of those to whom your manager is a peer. Get organization charts of your peers and their peers in other support areas that work directly with them and possibly you as well.

2. You need to get the job descriptions of every person on your team. If there is a variation in title, there needs to be a job description in place. Performing an in depth analysis of the job roles could mean you will have more to do if their job descriptions are more than 2 years old.

3. Get a copy of your budget! You need to know your NIE (non-interest expense) and your capital forecasted spend. And see if you can get last year's budget and actual spend so you have an early source of comparison to find out where your team is relative to where they think they should be. Insist on having a running review (each month) of your variances, which are line items like salaries, rental items, etc. with a year to date comparison of what was forecasted

versus what actually happened. You need to know why anything is out of alignment by more than 5% - either way. It is your job to assure departmental consistency in your current spend, as well as your forecasted spend. The charge back or transit numbers are for your reference to budget. For example, if you see that transit number 9767 is constantly running over the forecast then you need to sit with that person and find out why, so it can be either explained or corrected.

4. Summary document of holidays and the vacation entitlement of your team – individually and in total. I assumed responsibility for a team the average tenure was just less than 10 years. The total vacation entitlement was equal to three man-years of time off. This meant that we had people off in key times of the year that saw no backup if there was a problem – not good. You need to determine if the same impact exists for your team.

5. You need to gain access to the employee evaluation reports for your staff, for the last two years. If there are any surprises, you need to know about them right away rather than 3-6 months from now. You should have these when you perform your one-on-one sessions. It is imperative to have them in hand when you walk in the door for the first time with each employee. Salary reviews can tip you off as to whether this person is a performer – or has seen some performance issues in the last 2 years.

6. Request a complete list of your team showing individual birth month and day, company anniversary date, salary, last increase and department charge back numbers. Then enter the birth date and anniversary date on your e-mail calendar so you can send them a note or drop in and see them when either occurs. If you want to earn the respect of your team, they need to know you care about them. The charge back numbers are your source of survival as a

manager – it reflects the total cost of ownership of your team and all budgets are based on approved forecasted costs.

7. A floor plan indicating where your people reside and any other space you are being charged for – or any space you may happen to support. If your team is growing, you need to determine in advance if there is a growth issue or not. Chances are good that your employees will not appreciate having their desk placed in a foyer or lobby because you forgot to plan for growth.

8. Ask for your departmental asset list and a report of your fixed asset depreciation charges. I have seen where over half of my depreciation charges actually belonged to another department and that my predecessor had never taken the time to question Finance on the reports he got. If you are trying to manage a tight budget with very little elbowroom, it's always reassuring to know that your asset list can be audited without surprises. Keep in mind that there are several reasons for validating fixed assets. The first is the charges to your budget. Another is that it is a catalog of what your team assumes ownership for so you have a map or inventory of all that your team owns. Finally, there is usually a tax that is imposed on the company for all assets. It is a small amount but can be significant if you have a large number of assets. So, by assuring that the assets exist and are fully depreciated you can also reduce your company taxes by removing assets that have been destroyed, given to schools or sold.

9. Get a copy of company policies, standards and procedures – this should include Human Resources. They will be your reference bible from this point on. You will not believe the number of times you will be forced to go back and re-read them to assist in a decision or handling an employee issue. But key in on the last sentence and the

use of "re-read". It means you need to sit down over a pot of coffee one night and go through every one of them to understand all you can about how business is managed in this company. What you cannot memorize, you need to at least know how to find in the future. It will be your lifeline for continuing to be a good manager versus one who pays lip service and is basically ignorant of the tools made available to them.

10. Review all flexible expense items. This would include telephone charges (especially long distance charges), cell phone, fax, modem, DSL and ISDN charges that are directed to your budget, as they are company items. You need to form your own conclusions on whether the people should have this type of freedom? Is there visible abuse? Review company policy on equipment and services afforded to specific individuals (like pagers, cell phones, PDA's or laptops). Then make a list and research each question. Before you make a decision, ask your staff to see how they would react to getting more or less spending freedom. Prepare yourself for some interesting responses.

11. Ask for the RCA (Root Cause Analysis) reports for all critical issues your team was accountable for in the last year. If they don't have any, you now have a number one priority to initiate for your team. If they are not logging their mistakes, chances are very good that they are not managing change control either. You could well be at the center of a department audit in the next 90 days. Doesn't that sound like fun?

12. Request a customer list, any survey lists identifying their approval or disapproval of your team's service level. Retrieve any associated Service Level Agreements (SLA) as well. You need to know who you are servicing, how happy (or unhappy) they are and what your team has

committed to prior to your entrance. By the way, if you manage a service department, your customers are the corporate employees and should be treated the same way as the customers who buy your products. In some circles they are considered the worst possible customers because they don't have to substantiate their demands. Now is the time to find out if you have Attila the Hun as a customer.

13. Request a vendor and associated contract list. You also need to know what your team has signed. I assumed responsibility for a team that was supporting employee customers who were signing their own 7 and 10 year contracts with long distance carriers. They were paying a good rate of 6 cents a minute long distance charge when the average person at home was paying 10 cents but our corporate team had already negotiated 4 cents a minute. It doesn't sound like much until you look at the dollar amount, as they were a call center for customer contacts. The savings throughout the company was over $500,000 – even after we paid our penalties for canceling long-term contracts. Ma Bell wasn't happy but our company was very pleased with the cost reductions.

14. A person usually manages internal company awards in HR or a designate in marketing. Find out if your team has been given any awards – or were runner up to an award. That should give you a clue on what the performance of your team has been like in the last 2 years. See if you can get your hands on company provided awards that you can distribute to your team when they deserve recognition. If not, you may have to dig a little into your personal funds to provide little incentives that yield wonderful returns in the minds of the staff.

15. A project summary - active and recently completed projects - should be carried with you at all times. If

you have a team that completes projects, you need to know what they did and how well they did it. You also need to know what is active and how close to being on schedule they are. Not meeting deadlines is sometimes a departmental disease. It sometimes takes little or no effort to stay on schedule. The best resource you can manage is person hours. Like money, you only have so much of it but unlike money, if you need more there are few ways of getting more.

16. Catalog contact phone numbers – office, home and emergency access pagers and cell phones. If you have to enact a Business Recovery exercise, you need to know where everyone is. This is especially important for those who are on call 7 X 24. If you can reach anyone at any time, you have your fingertips on the pulse of your team. Use it only when you have to and never abuse it. If you want to gain their trust, treat their time as if it were your own.

17. Verify signing authorization (delegated authority) for yourself and your direct reports. Every department has to have a process that allows invoices to be processed quickly. Delay leads to arrears and nobody wants to have a poor payment rapport with their vendors. Make certain that there is someone available to manage your signature process in your absence (your boss, a peer, etc.). By doing that, your team will never be in a position of compromise if they need a fast signature to resolve a very big problem. Also, be sure that there is enough authorization in place for each of your direct reports. If you have (for example) $100,000 delegated authority for expense items, you need to be sure that each of your managers has a percentage of your authorization and that Finance approves of the same.

You now have your reference source list and soon you will be bombarded with the results of your requests. It is imperative that you read and understand everything. You need to house that information in your head so you can repeat it in meetings. This is your vehicle to success in that everything you learn will establish credibility later. You now need to prioritize your reading and begin creating your plans to succeed. Your staff will see who and what you are the day you walk in.

Chapter Three – What are the Rules?

"Always follow the golden rule – even if you can't remember it at the time".

If you think you can manage a body of people without knowing what the rules are, you are sadly mistaken. You need to know what is expected of you by many of your organizational officers, beginning with your boss.

Now, I would hope that you and your boss (your manager) had a good heart to heart of what your role is supposed to be and how you need to fill that role. He or she should have explained what you are expected to accomplish in your first 90days, 6 months and possibly 1 year. You are probably not ready to look at a 2-5 year forecast.

If that has not happened, you need to make it happen or you are playing a game without knowing the rules and I guarantee, you will lose. Here they are in summary:

- What is expected of you from your manager
- What is expected of your team by your manager
- What your team expects from you
- What your department expects from you
- What HR expects from you
- What Finance expects from you
- What IT expects from you

- What Facilities expects from you
- What your customer (internal or external) expects from you (service level)
- What your government expects from you (regulatory if it applies)
- What the Communications department expects from you
- What the law expects from you.

You probably noticed that there is no entry for what you expect from everyone else. You have to build that on your own. Since you are new to management, you will soon learn how you must relate to each group so you too can do your job. But for now, let's look at each of them.

Your Manager

Your manager must put together a document – hand written or otherwise – of what is expected of you when you begin your job. It is imperative that the two of you work from that document each time you meet to do your reviews. "Review?" you say! This is when you and he or she sit down and review your last week and what you accomplished or did not accomplish. You then put together a plan for next week and at the end of that week, you review again. You need this in order to determine if you can meet the expectations or if you and your manager need to talk about how your expectation list is either inflated or reduced to allow you to meet expectations.

Inside that list should be the expectations of your team, by your manager. You need to see project lists, production guidelines, service level agreements (if they exist) and the status of any issues with people, production or projects. How else can you assume responsibility if you are not current with the achievements and problems? All of this should feed into a performance review that takes place annually – or possibly every 6 months. This vehicle should have the corporate objectives as well as those of your management. Attached to those, should be your personal objectives which you and your manager should have reviewed and both signed as being acceptable goals for you.

<u>Your Team</u>

You may have to wait until you talk with your team members, but it would be great if your boss had a list or summary of what your team needs from you. This may be basic like "Direction, Support and Leadership" or it may be more specific like reducing defective parts, increasing customer service or even reorganizing so that the team has a better rapport with the company in general. That last one is a dandy and frankly I love the challenges that live under those issues. But as a first time manager, it is somewhat like feeding the lions, with your feet. You do that once and you have no way to escape.

Your team is the mirror reflection of you. They emulate what you drive them to accomplish. If you are sensitive to customer issues, they will be courteous and considerate. If you want only fast response times and short telephone calls, they will be curt and insensitive. However, if you let them build a rapport with the customer and resolve problems with an attitude of preventing them from happening again, you can accomplish both without losing the customer.

So look in the mirror – but be careful, you need to see what is really there and not what you believe to be there.

I can remember (years ago) walking into the office of a CFO for a large pet food company and he was extremely upset with my company for messing up their network and accounting process. They were having serious problems getting the on line inventory to work properly and once entered, the chances of processing it in one night was slim to none. I came in with no preconceived ideas – thank goodness. If I had allowed my engineering team to lead me I would have assumed the problem was in the people of this very profitable company. Instead, I found that there was a problem with one person, the IT development manager who was over his head. At the same time, I had the local telephone company re-route the communications lines through different states to see where the problem was with the file transfer and on line updates. After six hours of testing, we found that the problem was in the code created by the customer. A couple of changes later, the application was running like a charm.

I sat with the CFO and explained that the application problem was resolved and that it was originated by some bad code. As for the nightly processing, it was caused by a very poor design and the changes I suggested were incorporated by the second in command and the process now ran in four hours instead of 16 hours.

When the CFO realized that he had been threatening our company for two months and that all the problems were his (not to mention that he had been holding invoice payment for 6 months because he was so certain he was right), he actually broke down and cried. I was so embarrassed for him I ran through his office closing all of his drapes (his office was all glass on three sides) so we could talk. My suggestions to him were to put the team in the hands of the young lady who made the design changes and let the manager assume his old job of coding – where he was quite competent and very comfortable. At the end of business that day, my company had retained a very important customer, a manager was now happy and a young woman was now managing a team that respected her a great deal. Win – win – win!

God that felt good!

Your Department

Your department has expectations too. They need you to assure that there is a cooperative spirit among their peers and their subordinates. They are hoping that you can come in and maintain the rapport (if it is already in place) or correct it if it is not. Your leadership is sometimes as important to your department as it is to your team and manager. Your peers need a form of cooperation that assures problems are resolved quickly; projects are performed with minimum friction; strategic forecasts are performed with total commitments from all teams – yours included. They expect you to manage your staff so there is maximum interaction between subordinates with knowledge transfer to and from each department. If you have new or critical information, you need to develop a channel that will release it quickly and only to the right people.

Above all, your department expects you to manage and control. Assure that your team does what they are supposed to do, when they are supposed to do it and with the highest efficiency possible.

Now that Gramm-Leach-Bliley and Sarbanes-Oxley (alias SOX) have been created, there is a new world out there that is watching far closer than ever before. We cannot allow the tragedies of Enron and WorldCom to be repeated so the pressure is on all companies to assure privacy and honest reporting are more than the requirements du jour. They are the fundamental backbone of every company. Failure to comply could easily remove your company from existence.

I have always felt that if I make my boss look good, I make our department look good and thus my team – and I – look good. Unfortunately I have made many mistakes in the past that I wish I could go back and change. For example, when I was with a manufacturing company, on a given day, I could not get any idea of mine through the head of the development manager. At the time, I just considered him a lost cause (just as he viewed me) and I worked around him. He was a very stubborn man and there were areas that he was not familiar with that he should have been – my area for example – which was the data center operations team. We fought and argued about everything and it wasn't until a year after I left that group that I saw the effects of what I did. There was little or no cooperation between the two teams and the department had an obvious emotional rift.

That department manager was not stupid – just uninformed. It was my responsibility to make sure he understood what we were trying to do and why we were doing it. If I had just taken the time to sit him down and walk him through the process – educate him – I am certain our team would have accomplished even more than we did. And we accomplished a great deal – but much of it was under duress. I was an arrogant bonehead that placed my abilities above his and my entire department looked like a family of ferrets that thought they smelled better than any of the other animals.

I can admit my errors now because I have had time to look at cause and effect. You need to do exactly the same thing and understand that it isn't important *who is right* – what truly is important is that the department – and each team – does the right thing for the customer and the company.

Human Resources

HR has its own requirements. You must perform all of your management duties as they relate to the Policies, Standards and Procedures (Best Practices) established by HR and the company. There is an expectation that any manager will conduct himself or herself as an example to the staff they manage as well as to the community. The best action for you is to read the Employee Relations and Personnel manuals from cover to cover and seek the assistance of HR when you are uncertain what to do.

You are responsible for monitoring salaries, grade levels and annual increases. If you have someone who is falling behind in their salary in relation to their work volume and required knowledge, there are several key actions you need to perform. You need to review the person, their capacity, growth potential and salary base to assure that it is elevated to a new level (when required) that rewards the person appropriately. That is, if your manager approves it after you have done the appropriate analysis.

You are also expected to manage your employee's negative behavior. If they are causing problems in meetings, social events or just failing to perform, you have to stay on top of this and assess their issues to determine if they need to be reported to management and/or

HR. If the issues are personal but are affecting their performance, you need to encourage them to contact the employee help line (sometimes referenced as an Employee Assistance Program)and provide them with good reasons why they should do it immediately. You also need to evaluate their performance regularly so that their education is in line with their growth requirements.

And last, but certainly not least, you need to provide HR with job descriptions that are accurate and contain the meat of their job with just enough fill (for example "other duties when assigned") to allow for some flexibility for both you and the employee. Remember, the job description is what you and your staff reference to justify additional staff, the existence of any head count and the level of financial reimbursement. It is far more than just a job description. It is a job foundation. Everything about the person who occupies that role is based on the description. You have a responsibility to assure that it is accurate, current and representative of the job duties based on the responsibilities and the subsequent accountability within the role.

By the way, it has become increasingly more obvious that the manager is responsible for the job role from the time justification is submitted and a person fills that role to the time the person is released from it – or if they voluntarily leave that role. If a person is fired and he or she questions the reasoning behind the release through the unemployment commission, you will be asked to participate in a review performed with the employee by a representative of the commission. The outcome will determine if the person is eligible for weekly unemployment payments. Have all your ducks in a row before this meeting and be assured that you are going to follow all the HR guidelines.

To replace that person, you need to be familiar with the forms and the process for the completion of those forms. Most companies have a process that requires three signatures for a role replacement and more for a role creation. A replacement will require your signature, your manager and HR. A new head is a budget issue.

Once approved within the realm of budget, you must have all the paperwork in order so that you can begin the approval process for role activation.

Then, every month, you need to report and manage your **head count**. A head count is the accounting of an approved position that is reporting to you. It does not include part time or contractors. Temporary or part time staff needs to be counted separately. If a role is eliminated, the head (or the person in that role) is eliminated. Your head count is the most important function you can manage, next to the budget. Completely understand what your head count is and protect it. If you cannot justify a head (or job role) it will go away. So protect it with knowledge and not with fear, uncertainty or doubt (the FUD concept). You must understand and be able to provide accurate explanation of the function of every role that reports to you. If you cannot, you may well cause the elimination of that role just because you were not smart enough to learn what that person really did.

Now, try looking that person in the eye when the time comes to explain to them why their job was just eliminated.

Finance

Finance watches your budget. They want you to forecast intelligently so that you are not constantly calling them to find out why you are above your monthly spend line. They will be calling you on those issues and you should be able to explain. Anything can affect your budget. An annual invoice that must be allocated by month can throw you off stride depending on how well you communicated this with Finance in advance. A price increase that was outside of your control (for example the price of gasoline) can affect your monthly report and as long as you can explain it, chances are good it will not have a devastating effect on your budget. I am certain many of you forecasted an increase of up to 10% for gasoline increases but were not prepared for a 100% jump.

Finance is always looking for capital explanations as well. You may have budgeted $100,000 for PC's for this year, but did you also base your depreciation on five years or on three? Usually a PC is rolled out after three to four years. If you based your depreciation schedule on five, you now have a hole in your forecasted expenses. Finance can be your very best ally at these times. They will work with you to assure that your assets are properly allocated and that you have an accurate fixed asset list to reference from month to month.

I assumed an area of responsibility once that the person had nearly one million dollars in capital allocated to his budget area that he knew nothing about. He was a manager with one employee and his function was basically project management. Their total assets were actually around $10,000 for PC's and printers. We searched the asset database and found that over $850,000 was accidentally miscoded to his general ledger account number. Needless to say our department expense budget looked much better – but unfortunately the person who actually owned the assets was shocked to see his budget increase by a significant amount of money. I would have loved to be a fly on the wall of his manager's office.

So here's the bottom line. If you can eliminate assets – especially if you can transfer them to someone else's budget – you can eliminate net costs. If the asset is depreciated, and you write it off the books because it was junk and had no resale value, you may still save money. Keep in mind if you own equipment, you need to be aware that there is a tax base that goes to the state and sometimes the local county or even city tax vaults as well. By eliminating that asset, you effectively reduce your company's taxes.

Keep your team lean and mean – it is best for you, the company and for the team as well.

Information Technology

IT expectations can be far greater – or smaller – depending on what you require from them and how much of it is hardware or software related. If you require specific software for yourself and your team, you need to expect to see a charge back of the associated lease/rental costs, service and support and upgrades. Many businesses are moving to the charge back world so that the "real" costs are seen as business costs since many more businesses still cling to the world of IT assuming all technology and support costs and subsequently being perceived as a necessary evil.

For years, IT costs have been exploding and there is no change in the perceivable future. The best way to manage costs is to make them visible. For example, I was getting a satellite invoice every month for our TV viewing that was over $100 for every month. It was not until I broke down the costs and saw that I was spending a significant portion of it on movie channels that replicated each other. By eliminating the redundant channels, I reduced my costs by 30% and literally lost nothing. IT costs can be managed the same way.

Each time I walk into a new role, I ask for the most recent copy of the department budget. It is absolutely imperative to me that I know what each person and every asset is costing the company. How else can I determine how we can go about improving our productivity if I cannot understand our expenses? By doing that I can better understand what it will cost to do anything. For example, if training & education needs to be elevated to increase performance I may need to look at head count and other costs so I can consider cost reduction in order to increase spending. IT is a great place to start.

What are your printing costs? I have seen many times where everyone has their own printer and the printer and toner costs are over $1,000 a year (for a small department). I can gain access to excellent CBT (Computer Based Training) for $500 by spending about $300 to create a shared printer environment and pull a bunch of assets out of our depreciation schedule. The result is a net savings realized for the overall budget and I am still able to spend expense money on the CBT training my team needed.

Yes, they will complain. Yes, they now have to walk farther to get their print out but nothing should change unless they justify the need for a separate printer – and I mean justify, not cry until the boss caves in. In a very short period of time, they will realize that the savings is perpetual and the money for training is now available every year.

There is no reason why each department cannot assume their own capital costs in that IT can establish the standards (vendor and equipment sizing) and the business unit merely orders the standard equipment and assumes all capital and depreciation costs. It sometimes gets a bit convoluted when it comes to service and support. If the business unit assumes the cost of software, should they also assume the cost of supporting it? I lean very heavily towards the "no way" response. If each department were to assume its own ownership, there would be pure chaos. There would be no way that the departments could be integrated into a common technology world. However, the advent of the SLA (Service Level Agreement) set the stage for the type of service and support that the business unit is prepared to pay for. This assumes that IT provides the agreed upon level in the SLA. This vehicle allows the BU to determine what they want, what they are prepared to pay and what IT will do if they fail to meet those objectives.

It's not a matter of getting IT or the BU over a barrel. It's a matter of defining what is best for the company and getting it on paper. Then you commit to it. It's kind of like saying "I Do" and really meaning it.

Facilities

Strategic planning is the key to having a successful relationship with Facilities. Department heads want everything yesterday and these requests bombard facilities every day. And, these department heads can't figure out why facilities couldn't read their collective minds. They are the people who can save your skin from being burned when you have an unrealistic time frame for change. They manage the furniture and fixtures, photocopiers and fax machines. They coordinate the utilities, square footage and all aspects of the environment. And yes, they live with the constant bickering of people in a common area – all wanting to control the company thermostat. If you want something for your team, chances are very good that these are the people who can provide it for you.

Over the years, I have learned that if you want to meet a schedule that is built around moving people, building a new or upgraded facility or reorganizing a team of people in a work environment, get facilities on your side and you are 80% there.

Take a good look at what they manage – for you:

- Floors, ceiling and walls
- Cubicles, offices and work areas
- Parking lots, building accesses and security
- Painting, carpeting, drywall and paintings
- Cafeteria, vending machines, water fountains and restrooms
- Photocopier, fax, mail and courier services
- More, and more, and more ....

Now, when was the last time you complained about any one of these items – if not all of them? I guarantee you that if you were managing these areas they would be as bad or possibly even worse.

When you are working on a major project that requires any movement of equipment or staff – call facilities first and when you are done – buy them a pizza or at least shake their hands because chances are good that they made you successful.

Your Customer

The customer deserves the cheapest, fastest, most reliable, best quality lowest cost item or service you can provide. So where do you fit in? What ever your predecessor did, you must do better. And, in the process of doing so, you must provide the best customer service they have ever seen.

So how good are you? And how good is your team? Have you inherited something great that has a high risk that the best you can do is screw it up? Or have you acquired a time bomb that is waiting to cause the next tsunami?

I prefer the latter. I'd much rather work at cleaning up a team than managing one of the best teams in the company. I don't believe I have the ability to improve on near perfection but I can certainly improve on the worst service in North America.

The first thing you must understand is that you are not the best person to do the job – there is always someone better than you. However, you have to believe that the best person to do the job is on your staff and you are the best person to train and educate that person to assume your responsibilities. They can then be the source of your next promotion, which leads them to assume your job. That is called succession planning. We'll be discussing that later in this book. Be it adequate for now, the meat of what I am trying to convey is that you need to align yourself with what the customer wants and let your team learn to relate to that and perform with the intention of elevating themselves to the best performance level they are capable of providing.

The best service providers are people who know people. They take the time to ask questions and dissect answers. They look for consistency in what customers want. They test the market area and find the right service buttons to push that returns higher sales and better customer rapport. It's kind of like finding that special itch spot on the center of your back that you cannot reach. You know what I'm talking about. It happens at least once a week and you end up using a spatula or a fireplace tool to reach it. Many resort to using a doorframe or the door itself to temporarily ease the wild itch that your body creates. And exactly how appreciative are you when you ask you friend, partner, associate to scratch it for you and after contorting your body to the exact spot that he or she is scratching, you finally feel the amazing relief of scratching that itch away. It's wonderful isn't it?

That is how a satisfied customer feels – especially when they came to you for something they really needed. You are the scratch for their itch. It doesn't matter if that itch is an online request for banking, a windshield wiper replacement or a fresh loaf of bread. If you can scratch that itch and provide them with what they want, you have done exactly what they needed you to do.

So how do you convey that message to your staff? How do you get them to understand what it is that they need to provide to the company to assure that the customer gets the best possible service level from you and your team? You have only two vehicles – awareness and communication. Learn what it is that your customer wants and communicate it to your team in such a way that they understand what they have to do to get it to them.

Working in the IT area is sometimes a difficult task because you are so far removed from the end customer that you sometimes feel that you are losing sight of the objectives. But that is where the IT customer (the employee) comes in handy. In banking, the teller employee has to face the real customer every day. And, when the customer asks for an account status and the employee hits enter on the keyboard and a green screen is staring back at them, life is not easy. I assure you, they know exactly what the customer wants – their blood!

Too many times the problems experienced by our employees are something that should not have happened. Accidental program change errors, file deletions, corrective reruns that hold production files from being available. Now compound that with Mother Nature knocking out communications lines and power failures, life in front of the customer gets extremely difficult. So very special people have to be hired to hold those positions. People who can manage pressure when the problems are outside of their control but also trained individuals who can think on their feet and provide manual alternatives that will satisfy the customer request so they can get on with their day.

Your department, whether it has front line exposure to the customer or not, must always consider the customer and the people in front of them. Your service level should be one that you would appreciate if you were the customer. By thinking that way, you will always be able to provide good service.

Your Communications Department

If you are approached by any representative of the media, follow this golden rule. ***Do not speak to the media!*** If you must say something either make it brief with: *"No Comment"* or advise them to speak to your communications department. It is highly probable that in your best attempt to convey an accurate and honest message to the media, it will get turned around and you will look like a fool and possibly jeopardize your future with the company – or possibly jeopardize the company itself. Be careful with trade magazines as well. They quite often misquote and exercise their right to reduce the message to something that will fit into their restricted column size. In the process of doing that, the content is either diluted or misinterpreted and once again, to your peers, you appear to be about sixty bricks short of a full load.

If your ego demands representation, try a pre-approved brief script reviewed by your communications department. That way you have satisfied your position with the company and increased the chances that they will print the entire source and resist diluting the content.

There are too many people out there in the viewing and listening audience who believe that they have a job to prove any article is wrong and every company is out to cheat the public. I would strongly suggest that you swallow your pride and let the people trained to interface with the media do exactly that – so you can focus on a long and rewarding career.

The Law

There are far too many entries that could go under this heading. Suffice it to say, the best posture to have in this category is to adhere to company policy, honestly address your internal and external auditor reviews and report everything – especially financial items. Respect your staff and treat them as you expect to be treated. Follow the corporate policies, practices and procedures and trust that you will never have to face any form of legal accusations.

Setting expectations is one of the most fundamental rules for success you can apply to your business or personal life. People enjoy being with other people who set expectations and strive to meet them. A good manager will live by the rules and not interpret them to satisfy his or her needs. Understanding and following the rules, for most people, is their source of survival. However, there are always the few bold people who find they have to really know the rules so they can bend them to their advantage. Others love pressing their faces against the walls of the rules to utilize every corner without the obvious appearance of stepping over the edge. No doubt, everyone eventually intentionally or accidentally breaks the rules – especially in their first year as a manager. What determines your longevity is how far you step over the line, the frequency and the attitude you have when you are caught doing it.

Oh yes, and one final point on rules. The same rules apply to you and your staff. Make sure your staff is just as cognizant of those rules as you are. Remember, you are accountable for anything they do wrong as well.

Chapter Four - Meet your staff and peers!

"Your first impression isn't your last impression if you land the job. You get to start over every day".

I personally believe it is absolutely imperative to meet your staff – all of them – as soon as possible. Face it, unless you are being promoted from the same team, they probably want to know who you are, if you are a tough manager and when they should post out or get on the web and start that job search. Granted, if you have staff in several countries and they number over 300, it may well provide you with a serious challenge – especially in trying to keep your budget in line. No matter how many people you have reporting to you, they appreciate seeing you and meeting you. By seeing them, you prove to them you exist and you provide yourself with the one major tool that allows you to align with them – a face to face verbal exchange.

It is just as important to meet your peers. How else can you gain their confidence if not through verbal exchange with a handshake and possibly a lunch? You need to understand that these people may well determine your next organizational move. I have seen several instances where a department head retires and when interviewed by the manager once removed, the peers nominate their associate. It takes respect, not fear, for a person to point to their peer and want him or her to be their next boss.

So what can you accomplish by meeting your peers as soon as possible? How about collaborative planning? I guarantee you that chances are good your predecessor was a person who believed in working with his or her peers and getting as much information as possible from them. It probably depends on why your position came open and whether they found a body under the desk or the previous manager ran through a plate glass door trying to get out of there.

Assuming both examples were not even close, it may be that you are being asked to build a new department or re-build one after an organizational change. Both will require knowledge you may not have right now. So start listening and getting as many ideas of what happened as you can. However, you have to remember to record but not assume accuracy. You will probably hear 15 renditions of what happened, what should happen and what they believe you need to do in order to get everything moving in the right direction. Everything you hear is fodder for your plans. You cannot make too many moves until you hear what you can from everyone involved. Your customer (or employee base), your staff, peers and management will all have varying opinions of what needs to happen to make you and the organization successful. It will take a very wise and patient person to determine what happens next. Don't rush – even if your boss says you only have "X" weeks or months. The first step you take will be the most visible and the one with the most risk.

Deadlines

I was asked to assume responsibility for a company that has a serious profit problem. I met with all the managers, my peers and our executive team. None of them agreed on what needed to happen. The person before me was very strong but with no experience in the role of managing the group. There were slightly over 100 people and nearly everyone was hard working and conscientious. After my preliminary evaluation, it was obvious that the organization had to change to allow growth without breaking the bank and of all the employees, two had to go. They were over opinionated and seriously lacked experience and even a general knowledge of the product they were supposed to be supporting. Demotion was out of the question. To top it all off, one other person was managing our business supplies and getting a kick back from the vendor.

For some reason, each team that managed a customer product had their own programmers, scripters, testers, operators and managers. Each team was completely redundant. Of course, this meant that if we acquired a new customer we had to build yet another team. Not good. Something drastic had to happen.

I reorganized the teams into a matrix and placed all programmers under one manager, all scripters under a manager, all testers under one manager and so on. There were some managers who had been promoted to fill holes and they were extremely new at their jobs. My work seriously increased until they were comfortable with their jobs, accustomed to owning their budgets, accountable for the success of their staff and ready to forecast without my 101 questions. Some had to be demoted because they were terrible managers and there was no home for them. All but one was happy to go back to their old roles. The one who didn't like the demotion sat with me and we talked about what he wanted to be when he grew up. Subsequently, I asked him to be the lead for the programming team – but not the manager. His job was to make sure that they developed shared code instead of rediscovering the wheel with new code every time we got a new account. He was the group technical lead and he did a fantastic job. He was even published later that year.

Everyone knows a standard organization – a pyramid with someone at the top, a few reporting to him or her and more reporting to them. It is the "standard" for silo thinking – and it works well in most organizations. My organization needed four areas of change (1) a flexible structure to support the changing demands (2) a vehicle for fast and accurate product development and (3) a means of auditing those development processes to ensure quality and customer satisfaction (4) above all – employee commitment and satisfaction.

Everything was accomplished – and more! After the first 2-3 weeks of programmers and scripters getting huffy over the fact that people in quality control were grading their works of art, they soon realized that by creating reliable and consistent code, they were soon getting accolades.

What is most important is why I chose the matrix. We had key customers whose projects required constant maintenance and support. We had many small customers who had "one time shot" projects. That meant we required two types of staff. The matrix organization was the solution.

Matrix Organizaiton

A matrix environment looks like this ....

Matrix Organization

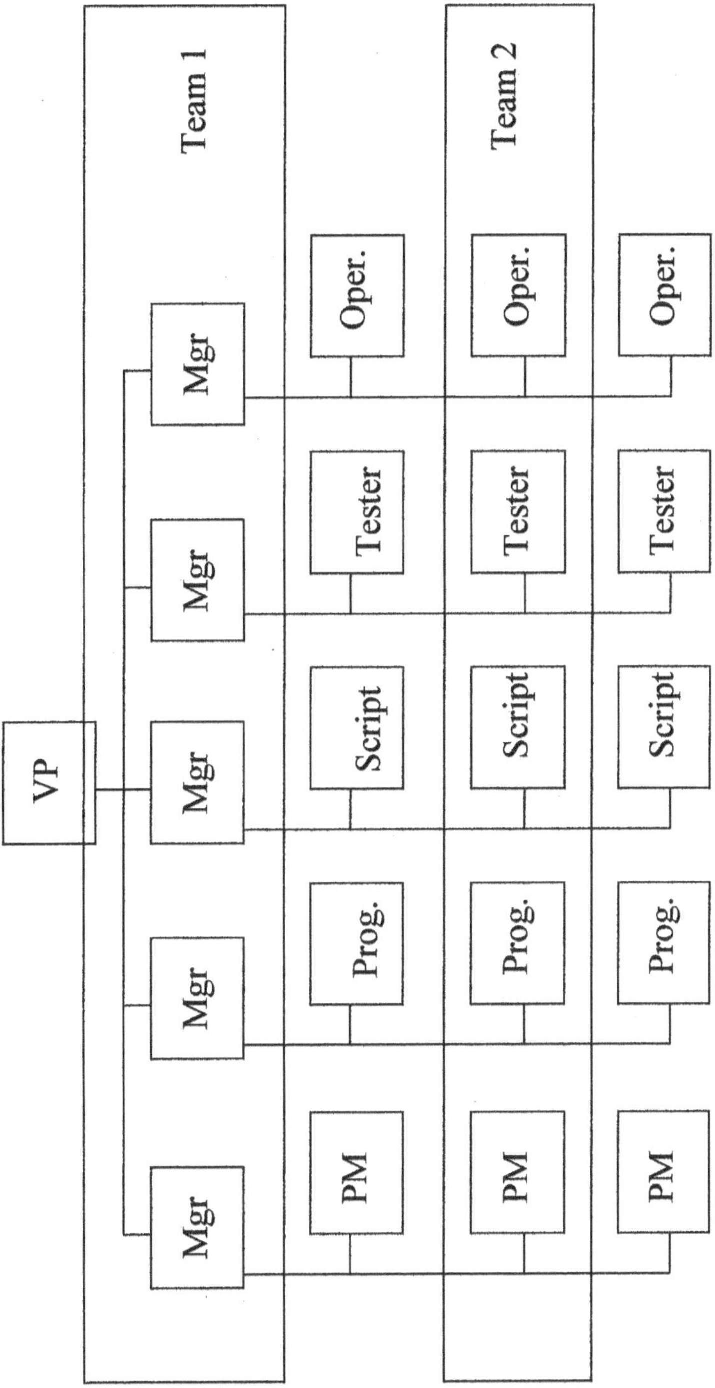

	Mgr	Mgr	Mgr	Mgr	Mgr
VP					

Team 1

Team 2

PM	Prog.	Script	Tester	Oper.
PM	Prog.	Script	Tester	Oper.
PM	Prog.	Script	Tester	Oper.

It involves people getting used to having two managers. One person manages their workload and technical direction and their primary manager must look after their disciplinary and personal development growth. The diagram is very basic. It shows Project Managers (PM) reporting to their manager while Programmers (Prog), Scripters, Testers and Operators (Oper) report to their respective manager. The PM then selects or assigns team members from each group to work on a project.

There are far more programmers, scripters, testers and operators than appear on my chart. The secret here is to only allow people to work on projects if they have trained someone to manage their daily activity load. This prevents one person from becoming the "gifted one". You know, the only person who knows how to fix a program and "save the day". It also gives the team members something to look forward to – a new project. In this case, we had very large customers with really cool gifts like T Shirts, hats and cute gadgets promoting their products.

Needless to say, everyone wanted to be on a project team so they could get some free stuff. Eventually, no one wants to be on maintenance so rotation became the demand of each person.

The bottom line here is that one organization (or size) does not fit all. Serious consideration must be given before moving to a matrix organization. It must require diverse teams, quick design and install projects and a competitive marketplace that insists on an accelerated speed to market (typical dot com environment). However, if it does fit, I suspect that you will be extremely happy with the organization and the results.

Change – it has to happen!

The key to success in preventing people from jumping ship or refusing to change was to provide a full explanation of the change at a team meeting. Give them a clear and concise explanation and open the floor for questions. Then provide examples of where the changes would be and what the results could be if it were implemented properly. In this case, people who had been stuck with maintenance now had a chance to take on new creative roles with new customer projects. It worked. Within four weeks everyone had gelled and the productivity went straight up.

Prior to this organizational change, major projects took 7-10 weeks. Afterwards, projects were taking 7-10 days. Did I listen to everyone? Absolutely! Did I implement everything that they suggested? No way! But I did implement answers to their problems and solutions to their errant processes that many of them suggested. What I built was no more than a solution to their documented issues and proposals. Maybe it wasn't as they would have perceived it, but it reflected the requirements of the owner and CEO as well as the ownership each of them wanted.

Be sure that you pay particular attention to the person deemed the "leader" or the most respected person in the team. Quite often that person is very quiet and prefers not to draw attention to him or herself. Yet they can provide a crystal clear accounting of the way it was before things got intense. That one person can sometimes give you the key to the problem without ever mentioning the solution. In my case it was three different people who were the production leaders of the group and probably the backbone of the customer satisfaction for the company.

One more thing! In order to accelerate the change process, I asked each team of people – excluding their manager – to identify a technical team lead that would provide the technical direction of the entire team. But, this person would not be responsible for the discipline of the group or the individuals therein. Their job role was to follow my direction and spend no more than one hour every week and create time saving procedures to be improved by the team and implemented that week. Historically, everyone created their own check digit calculation routines, their own edit routines and so on. There was no consistency and no time savings. Without the influence of a manager, they were now directed to develop "the best possible routines" to critically reduce development time and increase the quality of the code. Data Exceptions were mortal sins punishable by group harassment. It worked. User Acceptance Testing gradually became a mindless task with common 100% efficiency.

So where do you start?

If you have a problem determining where to start, I suggest that you start with your staff first. Your role affects them more than anyone else in the company and they are probably the people most interested in who you are and how you manage. Your peers are going to do their thing. Some will test your water (just like your staff) and others will ignore you as they can work without you. Yet others will extend a hand and provide earnest assistance in getting you off the ground and moving in the right direction. You have to be smart enough to be able to sort out the good from the bad and the really ugly. The latter is not the easiest because it has nothing to do with how they look – it is how they manage their honesty and whether they are trying to undermine you to elevate themselves in the eyes of their management. They usually have no idea how to be considerate and seldom are seen no more than three feet from the boss when he or she is in the room. The stain on their nose usually gives them away.

You have now completed your data search and have created a stack of notes. So what is next on your list? Gather all the information and place the findings into two categories and be sure to leave room for comments. The first category is "no change required" and I'm certain you know what the second category should be. Then prioritize. Chances are very good that the majority of change you may require will be minimal for many of the categories. Those remaining will probably stand up and scream "Change me now, or else!"

If you arrive to the conclusion "No change required for anything", then you are going to have yourself a smooth ride as their new manager. If that is the case, then you should have yet another check mark next to a new box called "Leave alone and try not to screw up".

However, chances are very good that something will require change for varying reasons and thus your work will be focused on how you will get from "A" to "B" where "A" is the efficiency level of the team when you started and "B" is the overall productivity level you expect to reach in "X" weeks or months.

So what did we just cover in this chapter? Well, we started with the basics of meeting people and determining how they are organized. From that, you can determine how to interact with them, resolve problems, build procedural processes and basically relate to them. You can better understand their restrictions and where the areas are with the most resistance to change. This usually allows you to better see the areas with open channels of communication – if they exist.

Knowing the organization also allows you to better understand how they work and where their decision makers are. Don't assume all decisions are made at the top of the organization. Some department heads can't be bothered with the day to day activities you may manage. So you need not waste your time (or theirs) because you can approach their direct reports with the topics of discussion. This knowledge should allow you to resolve problems faster and make changes/proposals to people who can react to your needs.

Good luck!

Chapter Five - Meet your SLA Holders!

"Great service is the art of meeting expectations the customer didn't know they had".

For the last 10 years I have been providing my staff with an analogy so they could better understand what service level is all about – let me share it with you.

Excellent service is one where you never have a problem and don't realize that there is such a thing as a potential issue. For example, when you pick up the phone what is the first thing you expect to hear? You expect to hear the **dial tone**. And how long do you want to wait for it? Are you willing to wait 5 seconds, 3 seconds or 1 second? You don't want to wait at all! When is the last time you had to wait for a dial tone? That is my point! You grow to expect that every time you pick up the phone that you will immediately hear a dial tone and you begin to dial. As a matter of fact I expect that many of you don't even listen for a dial tone. You pick the phone up and start dialing.

You expect your car to start, your fridge light to go off, your garage door to open and your federal government to find new ways to spend your tax money.

You expect every call you make to go through – unless it's a cell phone and you give the same odds to you recovering both socks from your dryer. But your expectations are truly already set for your next phone call.

Now that is what I call a high availability service level agreement!

And, how many of you realize that there are tens of thousands of people working to provide you with that dial tone? Of course there are the operators you have available to you at your beck and call but how many engineers and technicians are managing an electronic nervous system that competes with that of the human body – just so you can talk to Aunt Phoebe.

So what are you prepared to offer the people and the department that you support?

These are your Service Level Agreement holders. They determine why and if you have a job. Depending on what area of a company you manage, you could have a small handful or (if in the case of IT) every management team in the company. How well you perform is entirely dependant on what type of service level agreement (SLA) you have and how aggressive it is relative to the market and the capabilities of your team.

Today, there is a favorite term of "all nines" or "five nines" where the service level provided is 99.999 percent of a possible 100%. This is extremely aggressive but can be attained if the service or maintenance window is carved out and is adequate for the time frame needed to maintain the product that the service level is based on. Too often, a service level is established and the group providing the service does not consider what is needed to give a customer basic support. For example let's look at a network support team. Circuits need to be taken down to upgrade the circuits or the programs or hardware that provides those circuits. That service overhead must be removed from the service time frame or you have just set an impossible goal. Therefore, if you allocate one hour a week (for example from midnight to 1:00 AM every Sunday night, for service or general maintenance, the rest of the time is measured for 100% availability. If you did not reserve this time, any outage – even if impossible to eliminate – will show as a performance rating well below 100%.

Let's assume that you provide an internal service of on line reports to the Finance area of your company. You have a team of people who do nothing but design, upgrade and maintain reports for the Finance group. You would probably have a service level agreement that states you will provide all documented reports to that group every day by 9:00 AM. Well, what happens when you cannot provide those reports by 9:00 and the reason is that another department (let's say Information Technology) had a mainframe upgrade that was supposed to happen the night before and it is still down at 9:00 this morning? Well, you just missed your 9:00 deadline – even though it was outside your control. Now you have to take a look at your agreement and see what you must do if you miss your agreement time frames.

Some SLA's require that the customer receive a financial credit from the supplier (you), which could be anything from a removal of an internal charge back to free service for a period of time. This could mean that you just got a budget hit that will affect your budget for the balance of the year. It may appear harmless to you but if the result negatively affects your budget, you need to have a contingency plan that will allow you to offset that loss. If the loss is significant, you may have to experience a head count reduction if your budget cannot be shaved back to absorb the loss. Now, do you want to make sure your SLA has enough coverage for conditions that are outside your control? You bet!

Several years ago a past manager of mine asked me to come to Atlanta to help relocate and build his international network support team. Shortly after I came on board I discovered that we had an SLA of four hours to identify and repair a circuit failure (known as Mean Time to Repair or MTTR). Considering the thousands of circuits we monitored, that was a very fair number. The problem was that our average time to repair a circuit was eight hours. Ouch!

Small wonder the IT management in our corporate offices were looking for their pound of flesh when I came on board. Needless to say, I had to haul my butt into the statistics world and find out why we were providing such a horrific level of service. After two pots of coffee and several hours of pouring through our trouble tickets, I discovered that we were correctly reporting our SLA but we were not closing the ticket when the problem was solved. Instead we waited for the customer to confirm that the problem was corrected and then closed the ticket. So, what's the problem? Watch this one unfold!

We had a customer in Mexico City. Our network monitor identified they had experienced a circuit failure at 4:45 PM (16:45 for those familiar with the military clock). We called them to confirm the outage and validated that their network was down. We set to work on diagnosing the problem and within 20 minutes had confirmed it was a power failure at a microwave station and when the router was reset, they were back up. We called back and they had left the office. It was Friday but not just any Friday – it was the weekend before their observation of the Immaculate Conception. It was one of their most sacred and observed holidays. We received a call back from them when they returned to work – nearly 10 days later. We closed the ticket. Our MTTR was 9 days, 15 hours and 45 minutes. Ask me if our SLA took a hit that month.

So what was the problem? We did what we were supposed to do and so did the customer, yet we had a terrible net effect. That was because we should have been managing based on our return to service and not their return from holiday. So, we began keeping two sets of stats. We continued with the MTTR as well as MTTPR (Mean Time To Problem Resolution). The latter became our means of recording and managing our SLA. From that time forward, we stopped the clock on problem management when we determined the problem to be resolved but kept the ticket open until the customer confirmed the problem was resolved. If it was not resolved, we removed the time entry for resolution and let the clock run until we felt the problem was resolved.

What was the result? Our SLA stayed at four hours but our actual average was just over three hours. Well within our SLA objectives and I kept my skin. Oh, and the customer was very pleased.

So how do you start the process of an SLA? And where should it come from? For starters, you need to be the person to initiate the SLA. Why? If it comes from them it will be far more aggressive. It is also possible they have an ulterior motive – because they are looking at out sourcing the product you provide. So, if you love being employed, you may want to be ahead of the curve on this one.

By the way, you should always be aware of what the cost of out sourcing your services would yield. Otherwise, you could easily be caught off guard with a request that you and your team cannot meet – and that would not be very good for you or your team.

So start by being aware of what it is you are providing, what it is costing the company (your customer) and how you compare to an outsourced service. Once you have that knowledge, you can better provide the service with benefits that an outsourced provider cannot give. For example, because everything in your company is performed within the confines of the company, you never have to worry about information leaving company premises and subsequently removing the fear of compromised confidential information. However, you do need to make absolutely certain that your team and those within the company are seriously versed on privacy and that they are more than aware of the consequences for sharing information with anyone that is not authorized to look at it.

Now that security is in place, how about the cost of your service? You need to be intimately aware of the unit cost of your product as compared to the world outside of your little community. Since we are looking at a reporting agreement, chances are good that you are providing them with on-line reports and you are charging them by the line of data. If the outside world is charging a tenth of a cent per line – you need to charge no more than that or you are encouraging your customer to look outside the company for the service. And, if your management can see these costs rising as compared to the average costs of the outside world, they may look even before your customer does.

OK, your customer's charges are competitive and you have an agreement that allows for service and maintenance thus providing them with access times that you can meet – or exceed. So what is your quality like? Are you moving with the times or are you lacking in quality for various reasons? Most of all is the customer noticing a drop in quality or is it just you who can see the problem right now? And what do you plan to do about it? Or are you waiting for the customer to notice the problem before you react? I strongly suggest that you not wait for your customer to call you with a complaint. Your quality department should be capable of seeing the issue and reacting to it by notifying the customer and setting up a quality enhancement problem ticket. If you treat your customer like you were the customer, chances are very good that you will retain that customer for a very long time.

Let's see now. You have quality under control and cost is competitive and you have a service level agreement that you can meet. It appears that you have everything you need to make life wonderful. Or do you? What about tomorrow?

If you want your team to be successful for a long time, you need to create a growth environment that exposes the customer to new and exciting products every year and strive to exceed your SLA every year. If you have taken my advice and seen you grow your team every year then you also need to have a customer that grows as well or you have created a void. If your customer does not grow, they will eventually surprise you and grow overnight and you will not be ready for them. How can that happen? The same way your team did – a new manager came in and turned them around. Now you are on the receiving end of a customer demand to which you may – or may not – be able to reciprocate. If you have done enough strategic planning, you will probably be slightly ahead of your customer and respond with costing information and time lines that will make the new manager smile. If not, you may well have closed the door of opportunity forever.

Make certain that you treat your customer like a partner. Besides, they really are. This is especially the case if you are both employed by the same company and your agreement is internal. Be sure to solicit their support in creating the SLA, reviewing it every year and evaluating alternatives that potentially reduce their cost and your overhead. It is a responsibility you have to both the customer and the company.

The bottom line – once again – is that if there is no SLA you need to establish one immediately. And remember, customers are why you exist. If you don't place them first they will never place you first either.

Chapter Six: Your boss – forecast, direction and objectives

"Strategic Planning, in the wrong hands, is an oxymoron".

Most organizations require that a manager and their employee have at least a yearly review of the goals and objectives of the employee to assure the employee is provided:

- A sense of direction for them that links their activity with that of the department
- Objectives that are aligned with the overall corporate objectives
- Personal projects that relate directly to the corporate objectives
- A means of personal growth and development.

By doing this, the employee is assured an opportunity to grow and become aligned with the company strategic direction as well as expand their view and potential for personal growth through advancement and renewed job responsibility.

So where does this start? Your boss is the best starting point, especially if you are new in your job. Your sense of direction is what you will emit so it's best that you have a very clear understanding of what is expected of you so you can pass it on to your staff. If you are wrong, your team will look as bad as you will – maybe even worse.

Without a corporate posture, you are wasting your time attempting to guide your staff. The best you can accomplish is a sincere sense of frustration topped with a peptic ulcer from worrying about why your accomplishments always fall short of executive expectations.

The corporate goals and objectives should eventually lead to your boss and his or her goals and objectives. Then, it's your turn. You should have goals and objectives that support those of your boss. Finally, your team should have goals and objectives that support yours. It's really not that difficult. If your company has a goal of $100 million profit for the fiscal year and by the time it makes it to your boss, he or she has a goal of $2 million dollars (and he has five direct reports), your boss may well chose to set the sales goals for your team to $400,000 each. Your team of 4 people (and counting yourself as a sales agent) would then have a sales goal of $80,000 each. The objective may be to land five new accounts this fiscal year while meeting, if not exceeding, the sales quota for the year. That would mean each of your team members, including you, must bring in one new customer. Another objective could be that you plan to lose no existing customers. Therefore your team objective would be to maintain – if not elevate – customer satisfaction.

Stop here. If your boss has not provided you with a solid forecast of achievable goals and well defined objectives, you are spitting into the wind if you think you can repair their mistake with some creative goal setting. You cannot accept a skeletal or poorly presented G&O document from your manager. You must insist on a valid document that clearly reflects attainable goals and completely understandable objectives that can be parsed and presented to your staff. Not having it represents a serious risk. Most reputable managers will take the time to explain the contents and assist you, especially if you are a new manager. If not, you may have reached your first and last road block.

Your team now has a set of goals and objectives but they have no plan. This is where you come in as a team leader and manager. You sit with your people and together you plan how you will succeed. Everyone now has the responsibility to inject thought and strategy into the plan so each person can reach their goal – or exceed it.

Get Thinking of what you can do!

Start with a blank page and, if you can, an off site team meeting. It's always a better, more thought provoking environment if you can throw on some casual clothes and take on a planning session in a cottage or a rented suite. All of you are away from the office, away from the telephones (with designated back up personnel) and in a setting that allows your staff to focus and enjoy. Ask for input from your team for everything. Yes, you may well have planned the day and the agenda but let the ideas flow.

Make sure you have major topics that break into smaller sections that can be managed one at a time or delegated to small teams. For example, if you have a staff of four, break them into two person working groups and assign them the same task to see how diversified their responses are and how quickly they can formulate and conclude. Then let all four of them debate the alternatives.

At the end of your day, you should have:

- A list of action plans that support the goals and objectives your team needs to address. It will be your reference source for the next 12 months.
- A number of tasks assigned to each person with feedback expectations for the next meting which will be your final review before presenting to your manager.
- A quarterly review plan with measurements intended to indicate your success to that point in the year. The metrics must have been decided upon in the meeting as well as the means of reporting the results – a spreadsheet and/or graph.

- A personal notation you made of each person. You should have recorded how they interacted, who the clear leader was, who had the best ideas, who listened and accepted and who needs to see some personal growth to remain on the team.
- A separate note on who knows the company, and your department, the best.
- Your own action plan on how you are going to help each person grow to become better employees and possibly managers.

Now you have the tools you need to prepare their performance review. You now know where they fit into your team, who is to be prepped for succession planning, who needs a major personality overhaul and who is the creative brains of your group. Each will need to know how well they relate to one another and what they need to focus on for the next year to get a better understanding of the company and how they should be supporting it.

Now, one at a time, prepare their review. Start with how well they are relating to their job, their team, you, their customer, the budget, the projects and the success of your team. Be sure to be very honest, extremely fair and pointedly direct. By that last point, I mean you are not beating around the bushes trying to find a way to say "shape up or ship out". If they are not cutting it you have to tell them exactly that but also tell them why.

"Brenda, your sales numbers are down form last year and at this rate you have no hope to meet your first quarter objectives. Let's take at look at what is happening and see if we can find out why and get you turned around before year end".

You were honest, fair, direct and objective. You presented the employee with both an assessment and a new objective – making it to the fourth quarter.

Too often managers perform an assessment and fail to identify areas of improvement. It's as if they have a phobia about presenting what might be perceived as bad news. That is really unfortunate because you are leaving out the area that means far more than reiterative kudos to the employee. You are in fact preparing them for personal growth. This is the area that can well determine if he or she can be promoted. Let's look at that for a minute.

Kevin is a great guy. Everyone loves working with him and his customers ask for him by his first name when calling. He has the highest sales in the team and has a meticulous dress code. So what's the issue? He can't handle constructive criticism. He's fine as long as everyone agrees with him. If you don't he assumes you are out to get him or blow away his credibility. You, as his manager, have a responsibility to bring this to his attention. I wouldn't suggest you do it by pointing at him in a staff meeting and stating that he needs to grow up. I would, however, suggest that you meet him behind a closed door and address it as part of his performance review as a "growth objective". He needs to understand that he is not the only person with a functioning cranium and sometimes other people can see something more clearly because they don't have the emotion that he does when dealing with an issue. Take it slowly and responsibly. You are dealing with ego so you can't use a shoe wedge to get your point home. It's far better to set the stage with positive reinforcement around the entourage of good qualities before exposing him to the issue at hand. Don't expect him to take it easily as it's kind of like trying to swallow a horse pill without water. It may take time and creative presentation but it needs to be done. Remember, constructive feedback allows your team members to learn and grow.

Training & Education

OK. You dealt with growth objectives and you handed out plenty of kudos so your performance review is done. All you have to do is assign a value to their effort and if it's part of the compensation package, award the bonus.

Hold on a minute! Where is the training and education package? One of the most important parts of the review is what you will be exposing the employee to that will assist in their growth. Now is the time to define the educational path you prescribe to address areas of growth. Specific classes or reading material - or personal mentoring – could also be prescribed. If they have problems managing their day, give them a time management course. If they find communicating with their peers a challenge, give them an interpersonal skills class. Just be sure to address the issue with selective education that points to the opportunity for growth and allows them to execute it.

 The entire intention behind a performance review is to advise your employee how well (or poorly) they are doing, what they need to adjust to become better and what you are prepared to do to assist in the growth. Define or encapsulate their performance in the eyes of an objective manager. Present it to them as a concerned and proud manager. Offer them an opportunity to respond and provide points of consideration and listen like a concerned and patient manager.

You are molding a future strong performer for your company. It must be clearly evident to you by now that the only way that anyone can grow is by giving them the knowledge they need in order to grow. Give them the tools to work with that elevates their knowledge and also their intellectual property. And finally, give them the guidance that will allow them to achieve even more than they thought possible.

I have personally groomed several good managers. These were the same people that approached me when I moved to another company and I was able to re-hire. I have watched a college student grow into my job when I left a major manufacturer. He is now in a far more senior role working for the same company. I did literally nothing except to expose him to learning tools, challenge him with projects that tested his creativity and let him be who he was – a great manager.

Now, it's your turn. You became a manager because you were given an opportunity to grow. Make sure your staff has that same opportunity and be prepared to watch them grow out of your area and into other more challenging areas. Don't grieve at the loss of a valued employee – the company still has her or him. Admire their potential and be proud of the fact that you contributed to their success.

Chapter Seven: Get yourself organized – you're going to need it!

"Sage advice from a seasoned veteran is the recipe for success".

This is your make or break point. Your success as a manager will depend entirely on how well you can lead your team and get behind them and push when the time requires you to do so. It all depends on how well you can read your team and how organized you are as a manager to direct attention to each area that reports to you and provide varying levels of support – as needed.

However, you cannot organize your team if you are not organized. So where do you start? Try a Time Management course. This is usually no more than one day and worth five times the price if presented properly. Your expectations going in should be to receive specific direction on how to manage your time every day until you retire – maybe even beyond that. It is imperative that you seek control of your day to pull from it the maximum return on investment. You should be able to account for your every minute and report it back to your manager if need be. You should be able to break out your day into work sections (15 minute intervals) that are designed to get the most out of your day – other than back to back meetings. Use a time management book or an electronic version if your company supports it – even if you have to buy it. Either way, you benefit from being able to plan your day, week, and month and you can reflect back on it when ever you need to do so.

Get Organization-ized.

Make sure you have your organization chart close by for the first 2-3 months. If you only have a handful of direct reports, you can easily learn their names, job roles and where they report to you. But if you have 30 or more, you will probably need to keep their chart close at hand to save you time and embarrassment.

Get those business cards ASAP! Don't be afraid to distribute them and make sure you display your preferred name. If your name is Raymond and you prefer Ray, show it on the card. Most people don't assume you have a preferred name of Pete if your name is Peter. They risk alienating you the same day they meet you if they assume that and you don't agree. Give them to those who need to see it, not the executives you will meet. If you want to impress your boss's boss, know his or her name before you meet them and keep the card, their budget indirectly paid for it so don't spend their money and then flash it. Too much of that and you become U-N-E-M-P-L-O-Y-E-D!

Got a recorder? Use it! But not to record conversations or you will have to fall back on your mom's home-cooking until you get another job. Use it to record your findings that surprise you (like the name of your employee's partner or the names of their two children). Record your daily "To Do" list so you can review it before you go home for the day. Record driving instructions to the airport in Cincinnati Ohio (which is actually in Kentucky) or the closest dry cleaners or a great restaurant or your customer's corporate office. Then transfer it to a more permanent reference source like your electronic day timer. Record anything you feel you cannot remember and use it as a personal reminder for how you may well manage every day from this point on. It can well determine your speed of growth into newer and more challenging roles.

Hard Copy Reference Sources

Carry a personal bible. Not the religious kind (but you can do that too), the type of book that contains all of your meeting notes and action items from meetings. I guarantee you this little book will become your personal reference source many times over. You will be amazed to see how many times you reference it to back up what someone said, when you met them, what the reason was for the meeting and the subjects discussed. I happen to prefer a bound accountant's book with a ribbon tassel that marks the next entry page. I highlight and underscore every meeting name and date every meeting. And, on a regular basis, I reference the contents to validate what I have assigned to me from that meeting, what we discussed and key statements made by the attendees. There may be as many different ways to accomplish this as ways to serve eggs. But, you need to create or discover one that allows you to document your business life and readily access it when times demand it.

Depending on the type of job you perform, you may want something larger and more organized than just a book that contains your personal notes and a few documents. You may want a daily log of your year – or at least your month. This will require an investment and possibly even a course on how to use that investment. This reference source would allow you to assemble your strategic reference sources and keep them readily at hand for your immediate access, if need be. What would be inside it? All the things listed in Chapter two – your wish list. Once in place you can amend it as you acquire more reference notes. There are a number of very good vendor products out there. Be sure and find one that fits your needs and your budget.

"E"-Mail is in – sort of!

Treat e-mail as a means to an end and not your only means of communication. It's a great tool and frankly I don't know what I would do without it. I have managed many data centers whereby I had to communicate with people in different offices in different cities, states, provinces and countries. My staff worked 7 X 24 thus many of them had to be reached when I was not at the office. What a great means of broadcasting a new policy, monthly update or to schedule changes or meetings. But it does not substitute for face to face meetings and verbal message exchanges. When you find yourself in an e-mail exchange with a person in the office next to you, it's time to put down the keyboard and walk next door. You can lose more than you can gain by typing a "quick note". Besides, you can accidentally say far more than you intend because of perceived inflections, poorly placed bolding, upper case or underlines and the use of improper grammar. Go out there and shake a hand, pass on a smile and have a verbal exchange that allows body language to participate. Just be careful with that one – it too can lead to your early retirement.

I won't bother with dress code because today's e-business environment and corporate wide casual dress code has instituted a new level of dress code that still competes with the old business world of suits and semi-formal wear. What I can say however, is that you need to understand the dress code and make certain you adhere to it with no exceptions and that you are clean and neat. Once you have both of those in place, you are good to go. Appear organized and you present an organized person.

Watch your mouth!

If only I had heard and taken that type of advice years ago – I'd be so much better off. I have always had a wry (and sometimes extremely weird) sense of humor. Frankly, I never knew when to turn if off. A sense of humor is great – but not all the time. Business usually demands a serious mind and an exchange that emits factual foundation supporting a theory or poignant topic for consideration. Constant laughter or even poorly placed humor is annoying and felt to be a waste of time for those who are serious about the topic at hand, their time and the company bottom line.

I had a boss once who had superb command of the English language. He was an avid reader and loved historical and geographical tidbits that somehow always had a way of entering into daily conversation.

He also had a memory that would compete with that of a massive mainframe computer – and the same speed of recall. A pretty good sense of humor too. He had an uncanny way of knowing when to inject humor and when to be serious – he was a natural born salesman who absolutely loved his work. I never did pick up his sense of timing. Too bad, I have had many opportunities that were left behind because I didn't have that ever so key sense of timing.

Aside from humor, the only way to mess up your career is either through brain dead oration or Freudian slips. They both occur when you speak before considering the audience or the consequences and subsequently verbalize your own epitaph.

"Here lies Ray
fresh from the slaughter
when he eloquently described
the president's daughter".

I have only one word of advice - "THINK".

Know your audience and make every effort to portray a person with strong morals and a fundamental knowledge of the people surrounding him or her. Finally, don't make anyone search for a reason as to why you are there. Failure to meet the obligations of any of these points will in fact ruin your day – and most of your days thereafter.

All the write words

There is one last thing I suggest that you seriously consider as part of getting yourself organized. It is basic yet sorely missed when planning. It is of low cost but worth 1,000 times its weight in gold when missed. It is fundamental yet, for some reason, one of the last things one considers as a key item. It is obvious yet invisible until needed.

Now, have patience with me on this one. I assure you it is far more important than you think. It can determine your successful interview of a client, your first impression impact and your ability to get your client to agree on and sign up to your Service Level Agreement. It is a handy tool for your organization charts and considered a finishing touch to your dress code. It replaces e-mail and works closely with your recorder. It works even closer with your portable binder and your business cards. It's a **second** pen.

Boodaggle you say! Let's play this one out and see if my point is valid.

You present your SLA to your client and place an empty pen in front of them. You realize it is empty after your client attempts 23 tries at signing over the same spot with a pen that will not yield one letter let alone an entire name. You then fall into your dance hall impression of a full body search. Nothing! Needless to say, you have to fall back on the red magic marker you carry in your business bible. Nice touch. So tell me, why was it that you failed to get your bonus last year?

Here's a second point of consideration. Your client is providing you with the key reasons why their company is successful and their expectations of a strong vendor alliance. Needless to say, you are taking copious notes. The president is citing the three most important points of consideration for the products her company purchases and you run out of ink half way through the first one. How good is your memory? Oh, and don't try the recorder, it requires you ask permission first and you will destroy the power of the moment. Oh yes, the red magic marker – there you go! Let's see if the dark red stain produced on the other side of the paper you already wrote on will eliminate or at least obliterate everything you wrote down before you got to the three key points.

I won't belabor the point. If you believe you have everything covered without a second pen, just leave your best opportunities open for Murphy. The rest will be history.

Play it again ...

I mentioned a recorder earlier. It's a great idea for getting organized. Naturally you can use your voice mail as your means of recording action items for yourself, your blackberry, your Palm, your cell phone with 800 options and last but not least your second pen and paper. Most of these are options where a spur of the moment idea can be wrapped in silicon for a future reference. However, as I also stated earlier, do not assume that the people you work with, work for and hold as important clients will want you to have a recorder secretly running while they provide you with the details of their company strategic plans. ***Always ask permission*** and save yourself some embarrassing or even potentially libelous events.

There are a tonne (a metric tonne is larger than a regular ton) of electronic devices that can assist you in your search for the fastest and the most reliable way of recording, transcribing and shipping information to yourself, your company and your client. Make certain that you sit with your Corporate Security representative to see what is permitted by corporate governance. It is wise to have that information under your belt before starting that Radio Shack or Best Buy shopping spree. The results could be expensive if you buy a product that is not supported or worse yet, not permitted, by Corporate Security.

Ready, Fire, Aim!

No, this is not a type-o! It is what occurs when you do something in the wrong sequence and mess up the results. It's kind of like stirring the cookie dough after you baked it. So you need to change your sequence in order to see the results you expect. So how can you make certain that you don't make too many of those mistakes?

For starters, you now have the tools in hand to best support your needs as a manager. Use them wisely. You have an opportunity to turn your ambition into a rocketing career path and the only thing that can prevent you from reaching that success is yourself. Use your head and develop a daily habit of building your day – every day.

Plan your activities and include your staff as part of your activity. You have the responsibility of evaluating their performance at least once a year. Make time for them so you can properly monitor their growth.

Spend a proportional amount of your day for strategic planning which includes **Retrospective Evaluations** – of you. What did you do that met, exceeded or missed your objectives that day? What are you going to do to make up for your loss or accelerate your gain? Is your staff in front of you or behind you? Where are they supposed to be? What is your next step to guarantee the proper balance in the relationship between your actual and your forecast? Daily is probably too frequent unless you are in sales. However, you should do this at least once a week. Don't push it off for an extra day or week. Soon, you will stop doing it altogether. The return on investment of time is huge in that it allows you to see something very clearly – how well you are assuming this new role as manager.

It should be obvious to you that being a manager isn't what it used to be a few decades ago. Back then, you could get by with regurgitated marketing jargon, enough knowledge to fool yourself and an uncle who felt he should keep you employed for your mother's sake. Today, you succeed if you are organized, aggressive, conscientious and completely capable of performing the job. You have to be at least one step ahead of your sharpest direct report and on the heels of your executive and customers. Never doubt your ability unless you are trying to get by on your good looks or that uncle I was talking about.

Once you have developed a process that works, stick to it and always look at ways to refine it and prove to yourself that it is actually working. You are constantly being watched by your staff, your peers and your management. Think of it as frequent still shots of you compared to anyone else who is seen to be a rising star (or a bumbling idiot). The real question is whether they are trying to be more like you or checking out your armor for cracks.

Paranoia will lead to sleepless nights and consternation for you and your friends and family. Skilled repeatable processes are the source to a successful career. Read anything you can on those who can positively influence your career. Then take the best of what they offer and then, finally, just plain begin to execute.

Chapter Eight: Time Out
– Where are you now?!

"Each of us is looking for direction – the real test is in knowing how to ask for it?"

Let's see! You have a pocket full of organization charts along with your job description. You also have your wish list of key information about your job and how it relates to the rest of the company. You know the rules and you have met your staff. You met your service level agreement holders. Your boss has walked you through the organization and department goals and objectives so that you could plan your department goals and objectives. And you got yourself organized so you can take on literally any task.

All of this is nothing more than something to fill a series of binders or a high memory flash card if you don't have the drive to make a difference.

Assess your material, your knowledge base and your personal intestinal fortitude to "get the job done". If you don't have the air of someone who is driven to make a difference, you will have already conveyed that message to your staff, your manager and your customers.

So what could you possibly need in order to start effectively performing your job? How about the right attitude?

You are about to venture into a job role that is new to you but not to your staff. They had a manager before you and he or she was:

- Effective/ineffective
- Respected/not respected
- Amiable/a tyrant
- Responsible/Unaccountable
- Visionary/Near sighted
- Strong/Weak
- Aggressive/Non-confrontational
- Loud/meek
- Objective/Scatter brained
- Friendly/Self serving
- Focused/Aloof
- Cheerful/Grumpy
- Fair/Biased
- On/and on

.... Or, was he/she somewhere in the middle of all of these. So what should you do differently? I strongly suggest that you find out. The opinion of your management, your staff, your peers and your customers should provide you with two answers on each point of response. First, was he/she loved or hated and second, who loved or hated him or her.

If you get a mixed bag, don't be surprised because everyone likes something different depending on what they are after. For example your customers want someone who provides everything they want for a fair price – free is even better. Your management wants someone who will satisfy the customer without giving away the farm. Your peers want a person who is prepared to help them when they need it and stay out of their business. Employees want someone who is fair and forgiving, blind, stupid and wants to promote everyone with a 50% salary increase.

Your journey to success requires the same preparation as someone attempting to climb Mount Kilimanjaro. Success is based on intricate planning, flawless execution and plenty of information to support the first two. It wouldn't hurt to have a contingency plan. No matter how certain you are that you are going to be successful, it may be on your second or third try and not your first try. Don't let your ego get in the way of reality – the latter always wins.

How's your attitude?

There's an interesting point – your ego. Just why is it that you are attempting to become a manager? At this point you are well beyond serious consideration. You have made a commitment to actually become a manager. You are reading this text to get a rough idea of what you should be considering as you prepare. Exactly what was it that motivated you to go this far? Was it the expectation of money? Or are you more motivated by position of power or public image or the prestige of title? I would expect money with a drive for more recognition of effort and an opportunity to achieve far greater accomplishments than you have succeeded with thus far. But the others are completely ego driven. Those concern me. It doesn't concern me as to your drive or motivation. It concerns me in that you are going to have a direct effect on the success of others. And if your frame of mind is such that you are entirely focused on yourself, you may well destroy the opportunity for others so that you can end up on top.

I firmly believe that your success will be based on the success of your staff. It's far too easy to make yourself look like a hero when your staff does the work and you reach for the accolades. The best you can get out of that is an angry staff and you winning the departmental butt head award.

You need to know when to be behind your staff providing support and in front of them taking the hit. It's far more than just the right thing to do. It provides your staff with a definition of good management that is based on more than whether they like you. Do they respect you? Are you a reference source for things that they strive to do or are you a reference source for laughs and the recipient of a departmental document called "idiot statements of the month"?

In the eyes of your company, you have become manager to provide guidance, leadership and governance for a body of people whom, without your direction, would perform well but not beyond expectations. You are the person that helps your team earn an A+ versus a B- rating. Both are very good but the A+ is what everyone shoots for with hopes of getting at least a B+.

What's your altitude?

I have seen several of my peers move beyond my management level. I have only seen a few grow to a more senior role and they brought with them a pocket full of people who could assume his or her role. To me, those are my heroes.

If you place yourself above your staff, you may as well hand in your corporate credit card right now because you will grow only by playing some serious office politics and keeping your face in front of people who make decisions. Any form of potential respect for you is a thing of the past. But don't get respect confused with management by fear. I've seen what management through fear does as well. It drives away strong leaders and those who remain do so because they feel they have no where else to go. Their performance level drops and their quality of work is directly proportionate to your being out of town or not.

No wonder people are often metaphorically compared to tools. If someone is seen as consistent and reliable people, they are "level headed". The aggressive ones who seem to prefer to walk through people are the "hammer heads" that avoid any type of personal relationship with their staff. There are plenty more tool metaphors for screw driver and other tools but let's leave those and move on to something more PG rated.

The secret to your success will be how well you relate to your staff as a person they want to be on the same team with, want to talk to and want to work for. There you go; I ended three phrases with prepositions. My grammar teacher, Miss Blaze, would scream and point at me with that crooked finger if she were in front of me right now. But the point was still made – if you elevate your staff before yourself, they will elevate you in the eyes of your manager.

It's only fair. The more you do for them, the more they will want to do for you. Making certain that you look out for their welfare is not an option for you. It has to be your number one priority. Yes, business usually rates extremely high but this is actually part of the business process you own. It's kind of like your commitment to fair play. You treat your staff like they deserve fair reimbursement for a good days work and they will look out for you. Trust me. If they see that you are constantly looking out for them, when they see you in an awkward position – like your fly is down or you tucked your skirt into your pantyhose – they'll either let you know at that time or apologize for not telling you. I guess the key here is to have a really good sense of humor because it will surely be tested.

What's your amplitude?

So what is your *"mental range, scope, or capacity?"* What is your capacity versus your current depth or knowledge level? Have you done a full person evaluation – *of YOU*? I would hope that as a new manager you feel that you have enough experience to at least cover the bottom of your learning well and you are hoping that you will continue to grow via:

- Solid mentoring,
- Specific corporate training & education,
- A great deal of self applied future education (masters, doctorate, etc.)
- And extensive body and soul absorption of the activities around you including the school of hard knocks.

That is what will allow you to grow into more senior roles assuming you apply your learning and make decisions that prove you to be the right person for your job. But, once again, you have to be open for learning. The second you feel you have mastered your job you will be proven wrong – or worse yet – proven to be a fool.

When giving a presentation to your management, you are expected to have done your homework. That means you read everything you could get your hands on relating to the subject matter. It also means you have conferred with your team and extracted their knowledge on the issues as well as their feedback on potential solutions. You have reached a conclusion and are presenting it as your team response to the issue. If you reach a point where an excellent question comes your way and you have no idea what the answer is – just say so and state that you will provide a response ASAP. If you were to try to dance your way through a response with a whole lot of creativity and some techno-babble, chances are very good that you just convinced your management team that you are a lost cause.

What does that have to do with being a manager? Well, once again, you are the leader of your team and your pain is their pain. If your mental range, scope or capacity hit a self imposed ceiling then chances are very good that when you hit it, your staff will hear and see it.

Your team deserves a manager who knows when to learn and when to educate. Assuming you have made an effort to grow, there will never be any doubt that you are the right person to lead your team.

Look over your shoulder

It wasn't that long ago that I was working in Michigan building a data center for the corporate office of a world wide original equipment automotive manufacturer. At that time, we were running really close to budget but after talking with the engineers, I discovered that we ran five day chassis dyno (dynamometer) tests for Chrysler.

During that time, a power failure would cause us to lose all the information we had gathered to that point. Imagine, getting to a point where you only had two hours to go and losing everything that was collected in a week. Not pretty!

Armed with that information, I approached our CEO and begged for $300,000 to purchase and install a UPS and diesel generator for the building. Part of which was for the data center and the other part for the engine and chassis dynos. I presented my findings and let him make the decision. He agreed but clearly stated that he had reservations.

The day we occupied our new office, a terrible event took place. Someone was operating a four or five story crane and was attempting to lift a large steel beam to a construction site. From what I understand, there was not enough ballast weight and when he reached the maximum distance out from the crane, the crane fell forward from the weight of the steel beam and the entire structure fell over. It landed on an electric sub station, killed the operator and shut down four square miles of Auburn Hills.

The generator for the Silverdome failed to kick in and the roof structure deflated. Nearly 10,000 people attending some type of recreational vehicle or boat show had to be evacuated. We were one of the few buildings with lights on that day. Oh, and YES, there was a chassis dyno running and no data was lost because of the UPS and generator we installed.

There is no doubt in my mind that this event could have been avoided with the right ballast weight. And, three years later, our CEO could have used the $300,000 unnecessary generator as a reference topic for unbridled spending.

I did my homework. My staff supported me with some excellent vendor work and pricing. I gave a solid presentation. I still consider myself to be very lucky! I was lucky to have had a staff and peers that supported me and fed me solid facts. I hate to think of how it could have been if they felt differently about me as their manager.

All systems go!

Let's see what we have reviewed here. You are level headed, well-grounded and you are also always ready to learn. You have cataloged all the items you need to reference as you lead your team and you have decided that your team is more important than the quality and cost of the clothes you wear. You will make certain that your team is looked after and recognized for their efforts. You will constantly monitor their activities so that management sees their success but not in the guise of your personal achievements.

I'm impressed! You actually have your act together!

You have realized that you are really a learning machine and from this day forward you will learn from everyone you meet – including your staff. You will lead your team like a senior peer and not an all-knowing god of knowledge. Above all, you will treat your team the way you want to be treated. And, you will do all of this for your team and not for some hidden agenda that will result in your own personal elevation.

Remember, your team is a body of very intelligent people who will soon learn to read you like a book. The real question is whether they will treat you like the person you are or the person you project yourself as being? It's difficult for anyone to lead a team when they are in fact a walking facade. Your manager will see it as well.

Your team's future is your primary focus. How well you grow within your company is reflective of how well you manage your staff. From this point, everything is up to you!

Chapter Nine - What are the management and client expectations?

"A client is someone you can't live without and periodically can't live with – it's truly a marriage with an extremely high divorce rate".

OK – you have just been assigned a team of people to manage with a list of expectations for you and your team. If you don't have the list – request it from your manager because you have no means of measurement or statistical reference to see if you, or your predecessor, were meeting the expectations. Besides, excluding confidential material, you will need to pass it along to your staff as your base expectations so having that list is paramount.

With list in hand, you need to sit down with your staff individually and then as a group. If they are also managers, then your group meeting needs to be with all managers and then you can provide a team meeting for all your reports once you have a plan together. It is that very same plan that will see you and your team through the first year together. It will also be the source of their performance review as well as yours.

Interviews – the source of sleepless nights

As you perform your individual staff interviews, be sure to get a complete history review to assure their personnel files match what they are telling you. It is always difficult to avoid making a decision based on how they look. I have seen far too many cases where the employee with over 10 pounds of piercing material on their face is one of the best developers in the business. However, I have also seen where the person, who insists on wearing suits to work when the dress code is casual, is hiding something and it's not under the suit – it's what isn't inside his head. They are usually poorly perceived by the team or over qualified for their job. What you have to find out is whether that person should be part of the team or not. Forget about the suit – delve into their personnel files and create an interactive environment with them as they may just have a chip on their shoulders that was put there by your predecessor. One meeting can start to address that.

Years ago I had an individual reporting to one of my managers that was probably one of the best people on staff. He was bright, intuitive, informed and very capable of speaking his mind. The problem was he was angry. He was negatively opinionated on nearly everything and would start an argument at the drop of a hat – or toque. He was self-destructing. I spoke with his manager and asked if I could address the situation and he agreed to let me try. I waited until we had a management meeting and once it was finished, I asked him to join me in my office. When he came in I pointed to the two chairs facing my desk and advised him to sit in one and place the giant chip on his shoulders in the other one. He was shocked and wanted to know if it was that obvious. I had been with the company for less than two weeks and advised him that it was very obvious. We began what was soon to be one of the best conversations I had ever had with an employee. He was open, caring and humble. To this day, I talk of this exchange without mentioning names because I believe I had to hurt him a little in order for both of us to grow. From that day, he mentored me on technology areas that were new to me and I mentored him on his management style and interpersonal skills.

The next step – your customer

Once you have completed all the interviews, you need to interview the business unit (BU) that your team supports. This is covered in the next chapter but here is what is needed while you are interviewing your staff.

This is where your success will be tested. As I stated earlier, there are a lot of people who think they know your job better than you do – the only real exception to this would be your boss. However, if the business units perceive your team as a waste of money and two miles short of reliable, chances are very good that nothing you say will change that – you have to change it through example. You have to prove to them that your words are not just words but rather a testimony to your commitment. So if you want a strong ally, bring them into your change plans and make them part of the final solution.

Wait a minute – I'm assuming you have a tough team to manage because they are failing in their jobs. What if they are doing just fine and the risk is more that you will create a failing team? Your interview with the business units (and your peers) will provide all the material you will need to determine whether your new job will be a test of courage or not. Either way, you need to know where your team sits relative to the perception of service level. If it is going well you have only two jobs ahead of you:

1. Assuming control without trying to fix something that is not broken. Look at what got them to where they are and then you educate yourself on what you will have to do to ensure a continuation of the expected service level.

2. Prepare a strategic plan that either embraces the previous plan or elevates it beyond customer expectation. Keep in mind that no one should expect to elevate a successful team in their first year. Keeping it humming should be your first action item. Your strategic plan should have three points of measurement – Three months (How am

I/we doing?) – six months (Are we in budget and meeting the demands) and one year (How was the closing budget relative to forecast and where is our headcount? Did I lose people or elevate them to roles outside of the team? Did my team get larger and if so, why? These should be referenced monthly and shared with your direct reports.

Next, you have to evaluate where you are relative to where you believe you need to be. This is the most difficult part as it's a combination of conjecture and a wet index figure pointed straight up in the air to determine wind direction.

Measuring Success – Your Budget

You have interviewed you staff, peers and next, your customers. You have an objective (let's say) to reduce cost and evaluate service level. So now you need to know what means of measurement your team has and take a serious look at what your current level is costing the company.

If you do not have control of your budget – stop here. There is no way that you can apply change if your empowerment is limited to making proposals. Every job provides the occupant with accountability and responsibility but the real element of success is based on what you are authorized to do. Yes, everyone needs to have a governing budget but how you manage it should be your responsibility. If you do not have that, you have been denied the basic area of control that you require. You are not empowered. Therefore, close the books and pass on this management offer. You have limited control and that spells failure. However, if you do not have control because your manager is holding it until you get trained – then I retract that statement because he/she knows what he/she is doing.

Assuming that your delegated authority includes full capital and expense control, you now need to find out what the rest of the world is doing and how much it is costing them for similar functionality. By doing this, you are now comparing apples to apples. But don't get all caught up in a detail analysis at this time. If you are managing an IT team, the best way to initiate this process is to have your arms around general information like:

- What are the costs per MIP for your operations area as well as your cost per tape and disk storage unit?
- What is your cost per terabyte of storage for your LAN/WAN team?
- What is your cost per server and cost per PC for lease/purchase, service and support?
- What is your network cost for data links and ISDN or dial back services when the links fail?
- What is your cost per head in security?
- How many projects are you managing and what is their success rate in meeting both cost and timeline restrictions?
- What is your program failure rate per week?
- What is your rerun percentage per week?
- What is your complaint call average per month?
- What has your head count average been for the last three years? Has there been an increase in workload or are you running reasonably flat?
- How many of your software, operating system and support software packages are running at current release levels or back one release? How many are out of support?
- How lucky do you feel?

The last one is just as important and its predecessors as your enthusiasm and energy need to be proportional to the number of issues that require correction. The answer to each of these lies in what tools your team has available to them. If they don't have them, you need to prioritize the tools and start submitting requests for the right tools to do the right job. For example, a comprehensive trouble ticketing software package might be the highest one on your list. That product alone can answer one of the most regularly asked questions throughout every industry, "What is my mean time to repair for program failures, PC repairs and network recovery"?

Service Level Agreements

I know we have already talked about this but you need to understand that this is more than a philosophy; it is the means by which you and your team will succeed. These can be either your savior or your nemesis. It is imperative that when you prepare these, you do so with full awareness of the capabilities of your team and your third party vendors. If you do not have full control of either, you will never meet the objectives of your BU. Place your head on block of wood and instruct the BU to swing the axe with full force while you recite from a book of your favorite prayers.

If they are not in place, the only thing I can suggest that that you do so immediately. If you don't measure your service, the BU will and they will be far more critical if they are not held to some form of universal measurement other than "I want". Their measurements will not be accurate but that won't matter. This is not a "Them" versus "Us" scenario. It is a customer seeking a support level that is acceptable to them considering they are paying the bill.

Building SLA's is not as difficult as one might think. Get yourself on the Internet and you will find that there are tons of people in the same boat as you. You will also discover they are more than willing to share their personal experiences with ideas on how to improve service level as well as report it.

Begin with the basics and build on them from there. If your SLA's are already in place but do not conform to the universal standards, find out if they are too aggressive or too easy to achieve. From there you at least have a line in the sand that you have to either elevate or make more realistic.

Surveys & Statistics – your source of survival

Begin doing two other things – regular audited reporting and customer satisfaction surveys. If you can, make the survey part of your regular business day. For example, every time there is a MAC request initiated (Move, Add, Change) ask them for their feedback as part of your intranet application closure. If you are in Finance, ask them how the monthly reports were presented for them. Were they on time? Were they accurate? Then, feed that back to the department heads. There's nothing like a piece of reality pie with your cold coffee.

As of now you are ready to assemble your findings into a summary of the status – or state of the union, if you will. Sit down with your manager and make certain you have his or her support. You need their commitment to the numbers and their support in your proposed change. As of now, you are being measured to international standards. As of now, you are being statistically counted.

You have documented the status of you and your team relative to the rest of the business world. Where can you go from here? Nothing but Up!!

Maintain the momentum by having your team review the stats and attempt to come up with ideas to elevate the service level – even if it is just fractional. Any improvement is a good improvement. For example, years ago it was obvious to my desktop support manger and me that we did not have enough people in IT to support 300 users. So what could we do that would offset some of the demand? We looked for people who had the respect of their peers and the knowledge (or desire to acquire the knowledge) of their unique area of PC expertise. They were our administrative assistants. We then asked them to become our designated department support person. We cleared it with their managers and began training a handful of people on their specific applications and the hardware it was running on. They were also trained on the vendor hot line for problems and the key person on our team to contact when they experienced a problem they could not resolve.

Our desktop manager was very sharp and put together a training program she could present and provided excellent handouts with the two-day training course. When the smoke cleared, we reduced our help desk calls by 60% and increased our business unit service level immensely. It was a huge success.

To this day, I take my hat off to that manager. She was ahead of the curve on how to blend customer support into the work environment. Many of the people she trained went on to submit requests for additional software that made them even more efficient in their respective work areas. They managed the vendor interface for application problems while we maintained the hardware, utility and integration issues.

Today, it is very difficult to allow that to happen because of the stacked products that permit a software application to run and the tight relationship between IT and the software and hardware vendors. However, the idea still applies in that you can train people to provide their own software support if the proper relationship exists between them and the IT department.

Knowing your staff

This is going to be interesting. It's kind of like going out on a blind date and determining what you have to do to save the evening – forever.

Keep in mind that you applied for and were awarded this position as manager. If you have expectations that exceed the capacity of your team, you have two problems. (1) You are creating a lose/lose situation for you and your staff and (2) you are breaking up a team that may be very strong when lead by someone who knows how to manage them.

So, rather than declare the team a waste of time, why not see what they are made of. And, while you are at it, determine if the real task is whether the team problem is their new manager! Kind of makes the job a little more interesting doesn't it? Imagine, finding out that the team could have been successful with a different manager – even a chimpanzee with a speech impediment – as long as it wasn't you. That's the focus you need to have. When you look at a problem from the inside out, it sometimes has a settling effect on the person performing the evaluation – it brings home some reality.

Sit with each of your people and find out who they are and where they are from. I don't mean the country of origin – but the state of mind. Are they well educated? How many of them have associates degrees, bachelors, masters or even a PhD. I met an old school chum when I was walking through an automotive manufacturing plant. There he sat working a press and meeting his parts per minute quota. I asked him what brought him to the plant and he stated that his master's degree wasn't enough because the market wanted previous experience. He took the job so he could earn an income and then realized he was happy. Can't beat that!

You have their educational summary so find out if they have been in the business long and what other background they have. How well do they know your products – or for that matter – how well do they know your department and its objectives? What is their historical performance? Who are your shining stars and your dead weight? What has been the success level of your team – before you got there? Why? Was it the previous manager that set the successful or unsuccessful pace? Are you facing a losing battle or an uphill challenge? Or could you fall asleep for 12 months and come out of your comma with a winning team standing in front of you?

This assessment you perform will be the foundation for your goals and objectives – as a team. Don't get caught up looking for problems and fundamental weak areas. The problem, if there is one, could be that they are just not challenged.

There are plenty of books out there for you to read on how to manage your time, your team and your future. Buy one and start reading. As soon as you realize that you do not have all the answers, you take a dramatic step towards success. You may not find the answers in text books or "how to" sessions but you will certainly find out what other people are doing so you can determine if what they do – fits your business needs.

So where do you start with your timelines? How about working with your staff to set them? Is this another novel idea? Of course not! Where else would you get solid opinion if not from your staff? No one said they rode to work on glue horses so don't treat them as if you are the only person with some gray matter.

Measure Once

There are plenty of tools out there too. Gantt charts, critical paths hyper charts and good old Microsoft Project all do the job. The real trick isn't the tool – it's what you put into it and what you get back.

Unless you have a time and performance mandate, start slow but set the stage for a fast acceleration into strong productivity. For example, you are given a new team and a single statement – "Make them the best". Now that's intriguing! Are they the worst now? Are they the also-rans of the company? Are they good but not great? Are they great but could be superb? Please find out – your task may be as simple as supplying motivation or as complex as bringing them out of the 1980's and into the twenty first century.

Begin by documenting management's expectations.

Let's see what we have here. Your boss uses generalities like "it's taking too long to develop a plan to market a product". Or, "They never finish what they start". You have two issues here. The first is that your manager has a problem forming an opinion and the second is that your team is dysfunctional. That means you have to fix both problems. You have to learn how to get your manager to say what he or she really means and you need to shape up your team and make them more productive. The second problem can be resolved by monitoring the progress of the team assuming you can set a reasonable timeline for them to follow and meet as a due date. The first one may be the challenge of a lifetime.

If your boss has any value, he or she will have no problem assessing your overall team strengths and weaknesses and providing you with that assessment. Chances are very good that your boss will also have a series of expectations that you can document and use to build a timeline for you and your team. You will probably hear a statement like "You have six weeks to show a turn around for this group". You may even hear "This team has to be finished with the Scottsdale project by the end of November". Your potential of success or failure will be based on whether you hear this statement in May or the end of October.

Well, at least you now have an end date. Your timeline is established. Your credibility as a manager will now be formed based on what you can do in "X" months or weeks. So where are you relative to where you should be? That can be determined rather quickly by interviewing the person who owns the results of your project – the project owner.

The line of business or project owner (the patron of this project and whose hard earned budget money is sponsoring your project) will be easy to pick out of a crowd if your deadline is marked in weeks. He or she will be the one with the look of being possessed, displaying a full set of completely exposed teeth and having a difficult time trying not to drool. If they cannot complete a sentence or pronounce the word "ordinary", you probably don't have much left to do other than re-circulate your resume. If there is a sense of positive communications, you are definitely looking at a chance to prove yourself.

OK – seriously. Chances are very good that the owner does have problems and your job is to put their fears to rest so you can determine where you are relative to where they think you should be.

So what have we done thus far? We have learned what the expectations are for you and your team. Now you must set the expectations for your staff. If ever you have been direct, now is the time. Your team will be looking for clear direction and absolute goals. Assuming you do both, you will have your team on your side and the best wishes of your manager. Now, the next step is up to you.

Chapter Ten: Perspective!

"Just because you can't see it doesn't mean it isn't there".

I have always contended that if you can't see the depth of the problem, you cannot possibly determine the correct action to be taken to resolve it. Take a look at this diagram.

Perception – is how you look at it!

```
┌─────────────────────────────────┐
│                                 │
│                                 │
│          The Problem            │
│                                 │
│                                 │
└─────────────────────────────────┘
```

If you look at a problem straight on, you may find the answer but in more complex problems you have to twist it and turn it so you can bring all points of view into perspective. Otherwise, you will base your conclusion on a hidden view and the result is that you "assumed".

How to look at everything!

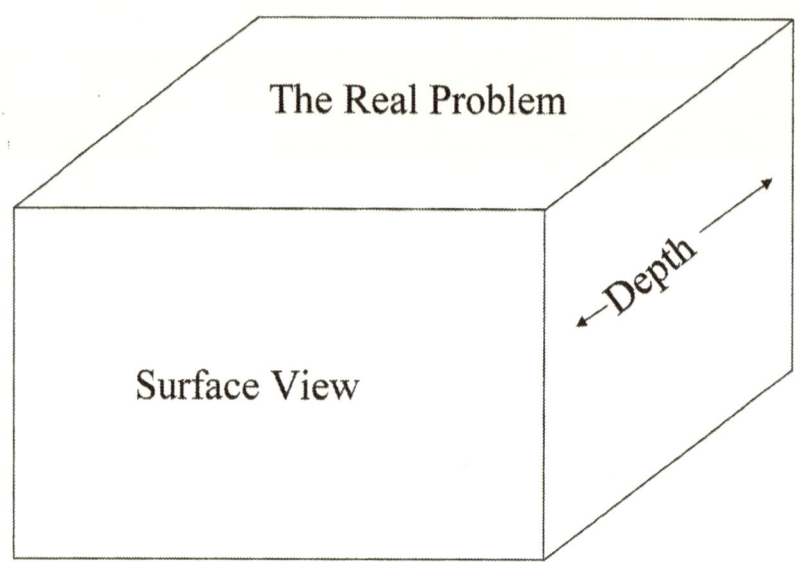

I often refer to this diagram as "finally seeing the depth of the problem".

I can remember talking with my sons about making certain that what you see truly reflects what you perceive is actually there. My oldest son was a college freshman and the youngest was two years behind him. They both looked at one another and exchanged that rolled eyes look and then returned the "oh, that's really interesting" gaze back to me.

I took them for a drive.

At the time, we lived in Michigan not far from Troy. A short distance off of I-75, going east, you drive by a building built in the shape of a parallelogram. As you approach it, it looks like any other building with depth, width and height dimensions that are obvious. As you drive by the building, perspective starts to change until you reach the point where the depth is not visible to your left or right. At that point the building becomes a single plane. It was then that I said, "Now tell me, what is holding this building up?"

The lesson was going very well that Sunday morning until the cars behind me, who were not particularly interested in my lesson, decided to apply their horn. They also displayed visible signs of being upset with the fact that I was stopped in the middle of three lanes. I guess they were on their way to church. My boys got the point, and I got the heck out of there.

Every opportunity I have, I will walk a willing listener through a process I experienced with an automotive company where the management was upset about the fact that we (IT) were spending too much of the company profit. They felt that we were overloading our capital and lease budgets with great amounts of money to upgrade our mainframe. Every year we were constantly running out of horsepower and having to upgrade again. To prepare them for what I was about to expose, I drew them a picture (Figure 10 A) of what our usage on the mainframe was really about.

This represented our mainframe with the primary applications that consumed most of the processor every business day. It was a 7 X 24 production operations that was driven by Just-In-Time inventory and profit ratios determined by the big three – not our sales force. Profit was good but not great and every penny was watched closely.

I don't know if this configuration was atypical of a manufacturing environment but it certainly reflected their environment at the time. Most of those present knew that development was primarily throughout the day and that testing occurred from 6:00 PM on into the midnight hour. Data Entry was still performed via terminal work stations that replaced cards and files were downloaded to the mainframe.

Daily Mainframe Usage

Manufacturing	30%
Finance	20%
Marketing & Sales	10%
Payroll	5%
Employee Relations	10%
Development & Testing	25%

Fig 10 A

I explained that each of the executives present had a share of the ownership of the mainframe (there was no chargeback at the time) but that each of them was dictating the percentage of utilization during the business day. I asked that each of them validate the percentages depicted on the diagram. Once they confirmed they were satisfied that it represented their respective activity, I continued - I then showed them this picture.

Usage after 5:00 PM

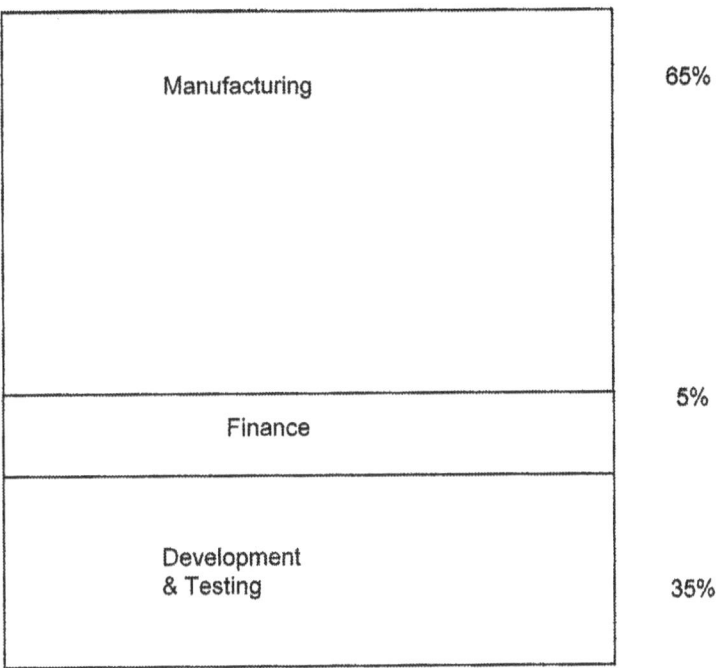

Fig 10 B

Night time processing showed pretty much what everyone expected. "So what's your point" was the opinion in the air (never spoken but everyone knew it was there). I didn't belabor the point. It is more than evident that Manufacturing defined the requirements; Finance had a bit of processing and Development & Testing rolled into the second and third shift – depending on the volume of demand in their area.

Finally I shared my last diagram.

Month End Demand

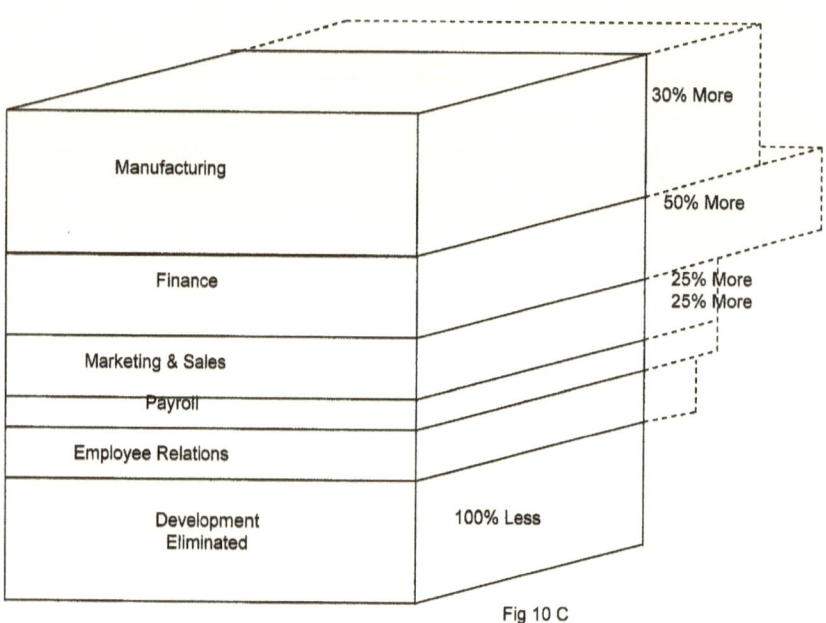

Fig 10 C

This three dimensional view (Figure 10 C) allowed me to show our executive that the machine had only so much power. The more we demanded of it, the longer everything ran. And, in order to push everything required into a 24 hour window, something had to be given up.

It was the perceived availability of power at month end that each person assumed was at our disposal. There was little comprehension as to what we had to do so that all the jobs were completed in time for:

- tax reports,
- shareholder reviews,
- business close out,

- Payroll and many, many other month end consolidation and reporting functions.

Notice something? Development isn't there anymore. We actually shut down the region and developers would perform other tasks like documentation, design specifications and other activities so that the production jobs could have their portion of the available horsepower. Some programmers began their development after midnight or on weekends to allow production to run. It was never enough so everything ran longer which is why the consumption takes the form of dotted lines. Typical of any man made environment that is constrained by defined restrictions, if you want to do more you have to either give something up or spend the money to expand the environment..

They finally understood the depth of the problem.

In order to have enough horsepower to perform the tasks demanded, we needed more and more horsepower because they were placing increasing demands on the processor – at specific times of each month.

That afternoon two orders were placed. The first was to upgrade the processor and the second was to research the report requests to see when and if they should be run versus prime time month end. Suddenly each executive had a new and far more accurate perception of the processing problem managed by IT. They were not necessarily the cause of the issues we were experiencing but now that they had a far better understanding of the problem. Executive meetings took on a new face – one where they suddenly began asking one another "Do you really need it on month end or could you wait until the next processing day"?

It was a very gratifying day for me.

So where is your perspective? Can you clearly see what you have and where you are going? If not, chances are good you need the Pope on your side in order to get anything done.

However, assuming you understand the meaning of perspective, and can see the depth of an issue, you are fully prepared to see your team through the weed bed of problems associated with shortened project time lines, head count freezes and budget cuts. All the things that make leading a team a true a challenge can be put behind you when you hand over your completed project to your shocked manager.

Chapter Eleven – Managing a problem

"A problem is as small as you perceive it to be and a large as you let it become".

Over the years, I have been amazed to find out how many people do not know how to manage a problem. Time and again I have walked into a problem environment to see the same thing – people getting caught up in the whirlwind approach to solving a problem and having no idea that they have little or no chance of ever resolving it. Let's take a quick look at it to see if you have been there ......

A person has a problem with a program, a design or a repetitive procedure. They eventually see the cause of the problem and fix it. The next day, it fails again. They fix it again and soon the vicious circle is in full motion. Failure is guaranteed because they got caught up in a two step analysis and resolution process. Here's what it looks like .....

- A problem is discovered and the person says "What happened"? The person listens to the feedback and looks at the results and then attempts to see what was wrong with the results.
- Once he or she sees the results they ask the next question "What can be done to fix it"? The fix is determined and immediately applied.

So where's the problem? The person is caught in this endless loop because he or she did not step back from the problem and ask two more critical questions:

- Why did it happen?
- What can I do to prevent it from happening again?

It sounds all too simple doesn't it? That is because it really is!

Now, take these four questions and put them together so that they are in sequence, repeatable and invoke answers that are correct and applicable to the problem at hand. If you apply them correctly to every problem you have, you will be 100% successful in resolving them. Perform them out of sequence and you will be back where our reference person was – lost in your own logic.

Too easy?

Absolutely! I have seen deer in headlight looks as I walk through it with small and very large groups of people. I am certain they are expecting the answer to the meaning of life and then I come out with these four small questions. It's kind of like getting to the last chapter of a large book only to find out it is part one of two. Not really what you were expecting and chances are good that you would disembowel the author with a leather bookmark if you had the opportunity.

Let's walk through this one time only and expand on each line item as we discover the mistakes made by many when following these steps.

What Happened?

What **REALLY** happened that caused this problem in the first place. You have a choice here. You can fall into the valley of assumptions or you can get all the answers from anyone who can provide you with them so you can draw a clear picture of the problem and the outcome.

Why did it happen?

Once again, this sounds all too simple. Yet, it is sometimes the last question a person asks when they are focused nose deep into a problem. The key is to be able to rebuild the problem so it is clearly repeatable. There may be a surprise waiting for you – it happened because of this condition and four others just like it. Amazing – you went looking for one problem and found five. Each one of them can cause the same failure. You just prevented yourself from experiencing four more outages.

Now you can move on to the next step. The one you could have experienced any number of times because you failed to ask why.

What do I have to do to fix it?

This is a fairly simple step. You merely put the changes into place that will eliminate the symptoms of the problem you discovered. It is a reasonably modest process that should provide little impact to the cranium and should also be easily documented (assuming you have change control where you work).

Keep in mind that the entire meat of this step is to apply a change that itself will not cause another problem. However, you are a master at what you do so the process is not only simple but speedy.

What do I have to do to prevent it from happening again?

Dear God, I wish more people would ask this question? That's why I underlined it. It is probably the most fundamental question to be placed in front of an intelligent person and yet it takes so much effort for it to be asked of oneself – or a team member who cares about being called at 2:00 AM to resolve a repeated problem.

The key here is to look at your resolution to see if it prevents the problem from happening again from other conditions. Let's say this is a Cobol program that aborts (crashes, fails, burns, blows up) when a data field expects numeric data and receives alphabetic, spaces or special characters instead. What is the usual process followed by those incapable of seeing past their egos? They test that field to prevent anything alphabetic from ever being detected and causing the numeric calculation from failing. But they fail to see the need for human error. What about zeros? What about high values? What about all nines? Would any of these possibilities cause a similar failure?

This is where you start separating yourself from all those also-rans out there who focus on the perceived problem and spend the next three weeks averaging two hours sleep every night.

You did it – you saw past the perceived problem and saw the real problem – there was not enough editing going on in your program. Rather than resolve the one problem with the one edit area, you chose to look through your program and elevate the capabilities of the program to reject all inferior data so that the program never fails again.

Here's what it looks like on paper ....

Problem Management

1. What Happened
2. Why did it Happen?
3. What can be done to fix it?
4. What needs to be done to prevent it from happening again?

Rather than getting stumped on steps one and three, you will now chose to execute steps one through four – every time.
Well, there is actually another process I use that has helped me annoy a lot of people and help many, many more. Every problem

requires that you ask a lot of questions and the answers determine your possibility of success. To make certain that I am working with people who want to contribute to the solution, I tend to measure my responses into only two categories. The first is a response that is reasonable and provides direction. Then you have responses that have absolutely no value for the listener. I keep a visible list of **"Ray's Unacceptable Responses"**.

This one could be a very sensitive area unless you are walking into a shop that has lots of problems. People don't like being told they are wrong – at least not to their face - and especially when you are the new kid on the block. However, you have to decide if there is a need to make an immediate change.

It will be tough, seemingly thankless and will move you right into the "solid jerk"" category **UNLESS** you can substantiate it with what you expect to hear in place of the specific phrase. Now you have provided the recipient of your statement with an alternative that saves face and allows a constructive conversation to evolve where a blood letting may have been destined.

Here they are:

Ray's Unacceptable Responses

- I don't know.
- No one ever taught me.
- This is the way we have always done it.
- I can't. (I won't)
- It's not my job.

I told you they were direct!

OK – let's see how one would work. You find out there is a problem so you ask the first person closest to you "What happened?" and you get the response "I don't know".

It's not only not creative it's known as a show stopper. It is a blunt response given to allow that person to wiggle out of the problem unscathed. So go somewhere – anywhere – except here, to get an answer.

There is an alternative for this person – let's see how this one sounds?

"I don't know – but I'll find out"!

Very nice! It provides the listener with many, many pieces of information. First, you do not know why the power cord to the fax machine is missing. However, you also stated that you are willing to find out and get that information back to me. It also tells me you have energy, you are prepared to learn and you have a drive to get to the truth. All are wonderful traits. And, it can be applied to each of the unacceptable responses. Let's try each one with a positive response.

Acceptable Responses

- I don't know … but I'll find out!
- No one ever taught me – but I'm willing to learn!
- This is the way we have always done it … but I'm open to new ideas!
- I can't. (I won't) …. I will!
- It's not my job … but I will do it!

Each one started as a reason for termination and ended as a statement of commitment. It started and ended with an attitude – a negative one that turned into a positive one. If only all problems could be put to rest this quickly.

Sometimes the problem has to be diagnosed in order for the answer to be discovered – sometimes the problem is right in front of you. You are expected to resolve the problem quickly, fairly and with the intention of never having to face it again. I guarantee you, if you follow this simple process of being direct, fair and honest, you will resolve problems quickly, with the help of your staff.

If you have to fall back on the unacceptable responses, be prepared for rebuttal. If you present it professionally and set expectations in that you will hold yourself to the same level of visibility, chances are good that your team will not perceive you as having an over sized ego. Always give your team a chance to save face – it will come back to you in the form of renewed support.

Good luck!

Chapter Twelve – Building an organization for today and tomorrow

"Team building is the art of getting one or more staff members to do what your kids refuse to do".

Probably the most difficult part of building a team is getting the right people to do the right job for today and tomorrow. It's kind of like building a car with the same set of expectations. You don't expect the car to be built one way for the next 20 years. People will get awfully tired of looking at the same car for more than two years. You also can't expect it to be perceived immediately as a classic – that is left up to the fate of how man cherishes his personal wheels. If you're lucky, you're still in business in 20 years.

It takes a special hand to build something that flexible, reliable and resilient. Maybe you have it and maybe you don't. But, if you have the right team, you may be able to do it because of their combined talents.

Earlier, I spoke of how you have to elevate your job so it retains its value in the eyes of the customer. It is more than a concept; it is a fact of life. So why can't you build a team with the same investment and expectations? Actually, you can!

Today, companies are trying to get lean and mean. Out sourcing and Off Shoring are some of the greatest alternatives to large burdened organizations. India has capitalized from this and will probably continue until they experience an increased social demand for salary and benefit packages that place the jobs back in North American soil again. But that is only one alternative.

As you shape your team, you need to make sure you have just enough backup to allow your remaining staff to have vacation, training & education and sick days. You also want to make certain that you have a maximum number of people reporting to managers or team leads. The days of having a manager with one report are all but over. And right behind that is the manager with 2-4 reports. Most organizations are upping the ante to a standard of seven to ten direct reports.

If you have a team of 4-5 direct reports, that should tell you one thing – you need to be in a position to assume more responsibility. However, you cannot lose sight of the need to have an organization that is quick on its feet and capable of having a chameleon like appearance to the casual observer. For example, when you get a peak demand in one area, can your team stop, reshape and execute? Let me give you an example.

You have a team of 10 people who each have specific areas of responsibility. In it, they have the responsibility to maintain something and keep it afloat. What happens when you get a special project? Do you assign it to one person and let that person carry the weight of the entire project or do you build your team around the project? How does your team handle a full emersion project? This is something that has the potential of over taking your entire team for 3-5 days – or more.

Can you survive? How do you manage daily activity? How do you manage changes? How do you manage peak volumes? And, how do you build a SWAT team that assembles infrequently and executes for short time frames?

Let me tell you how **NOT** to do it! You do not walk up to your boss and demand three more people and a salary increase. That's called an emergency visit to a proctologist to get that idea removed.

Special projects, SWAT teams and peak volumes need to be managed the same way you manage elevation. There are things that (1) **must** be done, (2) **need** to be done, (3) **should** be done, (4) can wait until a later date and (5) are no longer required. Handle them in that sequence and advise those to whom you report that their statistics will be late this month because you have to pack 10 pounds of stuff into a five pound bag. And then you execute.

There is only one way you can do this and that is by having a lean, mean "focused on execution" machine. You have a team of people who understand the objectives and know how to execute to meet the demands of the day and can keep the sequence of Must, Need, Want and Should in tow so you can address the demands of the day.

Keep this list close at hand.

- What must be done to meet my customer demands?
- What do I need to do so I meet the critical issues of the day?
- What should I do to keep my team above water and out of the jaws of failure?
- What can be put on the back burner to get me through the day?
- What is being done that is a waste of time, money or horse power and should be eliminated or assigned to someone else?

What ever you do, keep your team on the top of the list. They are more than your responsibility; they are your source of survival.

Anything you can invest in their success will yield success for you as well.

Now that you have your priorities straight, you need to look at what you have and what you need to do with it. The business world is evolving quickly and the demand for reliability, efficiency, cost containment and speed to market escalates every year. Because of that, you must keep evaluating where the market is and where your team needs to be to support that market.

Because of my age and my 40 plus years in Information Technology (alias Data Processing) I can handle being referenced to as "dirt in a shirt". However, it is that same experience that provides me with the retrospect of how it used to be a reasonably relaxed environment. Back then, I worked on mainframes that had 16 "K" of memory and a fraction of a MIP of horsepower. Compare that to the world of nanosecond response time today. WOW – now that's an extreme makeover.

One thing has remained consistent throughout our evolution – customer support. They expect us to provide them with a consistent level of service and possess a keen awareness of their needs. If you can form your team so it is malleable and responsive, you have the envy of all your peers. Make every effort to review your status relative to your demands. Always take into consideration automation, out sourcing and elimination when you see yourself at a crossroads for available horsepower relative to demand. You do your team an injustice if you assume that every load that comes your way is your demand and no one else's. You must allow yourself to view the load as an impact with alternative reaction areas. Maybe you can do it if you give up something else? Maybe you can do it as a leader while someone else performs the assigned tasks? Maybe you should pay to get it done through your budget without having to give up a head or any more responsibility? And maybe it should stay in your park because of the security and confidentiality requirements?

Make certain that no matter what the request, you react the same way – by viewing it as an opportunity to reduce cost, elevate performance or eliminate a portion of the competition. By doing that, you allow yourself to respond to each opportunity the same way – with a positive approach to maintaining budget, increasing volumes and elevating performance.

I guarantee you, if you address each and every opportunity this way, you will be a very successful and a respected executive well before (and after) the word **"retirement"** enters into your vocabulary.

Building a team is not an overnight task. You must sweat it out every step of the way. At first, you don't trust them any further than they trust you. Therefore, you need to create a foundation on to which you will actually build the trust and subsequently, your team. It starts with you proving you are to be trusted. You make a commitment and follow up on it. Then you make another one and follow up on it too. One false step and the house of cards you have built, collapses. Then, at some mysterious point, your team begins to trust you. It is all relative to how many times they have been lied to, abused and threatened before you came on board. Your staff evaluations will assist you in knowing whether you need to create a solid image of trust or look for a means of walking on water. Frankly, the latter may be easier.

How long can you wait to get to that point of being trusted? Depending on your goals and objectives, possibly not very long at all! Your plans have to be short and sweet. They have to be attainable in a measurable period of time and the results have to be visible.

Assuming you have referenced what we have talked about, you have created that lean mean machine called **"a team"**. You have their trust and they have yours. Now, you are ready for the really serious part of your job – calculating salary increases.

Chapter Thirteen – Statistics versus Metrics

We have already addressed this in a general sense but not the specifics of what you should be measuring versus what you tend to measure. When you start measuring your team you need to know the difference between collecting statistics and providing metrics relating to performance. Statistics relates to the volume of work you perform whereas metrics reflect the proximity to perfection.

Statistics

Here's a sample of statistics:

What you have here is a representation of sales by month and a summary of customer complaints. It reflects our sales and also indicates what our customers are experiencing. It clearly shows that our sales are declining and so are your customer complaints – but nothing else in relation to our customer service. So let's go out there and sell gang!

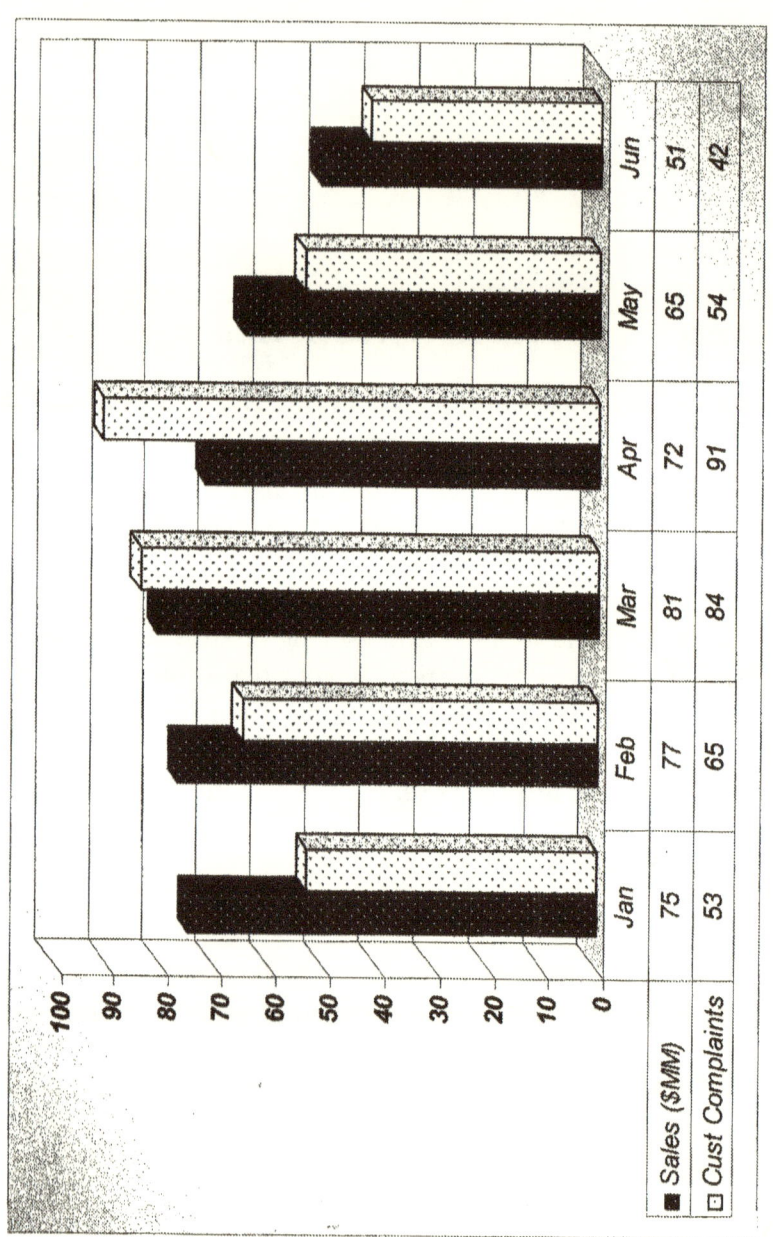

	Jan	Feb	Mar	Apr	May	Jun
■ Sales ($MM)	75	77	81	72	65	51
□ Cust Complaints	53	65	84	91	54	42

Alright then, if this represents statistics, what do metrics look like? For starters, they represent the frequency of what we don't want to do and what we can't do. They represent mistakes and how often they occur. For example, how many faulty parts do we manufacture? How many faulty parts do we create in relation to how many completely pass the quality and performance tests in the middle of, and at the end of each assembly line? Worse yet, how many are returned by our customer for refund? That really costs us as we have to assume the shipping and replacement costs of a finished good. Not to mention that we already paid for its shipment to the customer the first time.

At this stage of our measurements, we are shooting for 100% with an acceptance range of 99.99% to 100% reliable products. Tolerance is fine for now but zero tolerance should be every manufacturer's objective. Manufacturing 100% quality products with no factory floor defects and thus no shipping defects resulting in damaged goods, is the corporate goal.

So where is your team relative to this goal and how are you measuring it? It should not be much of a challenge for you to comply with this step of your management position. You are now responsible for the measurement of your team and the elevation of their performance to reflect the corporate goal of minimal quality issues today and absolutely none tomorrow. So what if you work in an area, like Information Technology, where the customer is another employee? How can you possibly measure your performance relative to the customer needs? Now that's an easy one – eliminate mistakes. Measure based on the **things you cannot do** and **cannot allow your team to do**. For example you cannot allow yourself to make these mistakes:

- You cannot cancel the wrong scheduled job. No detail required here – you get a choice here of severing one of your fingers to the first knuckle or being hung by your thumbs in the cafeteria during lunch hour.

- Identify the wrong failed part. There's nothing more rewarding to a field engineer than to get to a customer site after a long drive with the wrong part for replacement. You can tell if the person is annoyed when they eat the part rather than carry it back to their vehicle.

- Selling the wrong stock! Oh, that one makes everyone smile! The person that made the mistake claims he or she did what they were told. The one that was directing the activity claims ignorance and the affected customer tries to reach through the phone to find an available throat to choke.

So what are some of the things that you **cannot miss**? How about:

- You cannot miss a program termination or ABEND. If you do, many more programs will ABEND because it didn't finish properly. Or worse yet, everything will sit in a suspended state awaiting a response to the failed program. One problem could possibly create dozens more. And, it will force hundreds of lost programmer hours trying to resolve the original problem and those that were caused because of the first one. Programmers really love that.

- You cannot release a news broadcast without performing a proof read of the document at least twice. You must always look for spelling errors, grammatical errors and sentences that don't align to the story. Failure to do so may mean your viewing audience knows you do shoddy work. All you can do is update your resume and hope for the best.

- You cannot miss an emergency fax, e-mail or phone call that your boss is waiting for so she can make an offer to purchase a company. You therefore make certain that you have call forwarding active, plenty of paper in the fax machine and you have a redundant Internet Provider.

I believe you get the idea behind these statements. If you make a mistake or miss an opportunity to resolve an issue, the pain and anguish is ten fold. So if you are shooting for 100% customer satisfaction, you cannot allow these types of issues to occur with any regularity. Never is even better.

Metrics

Now you are ready for metrics!

You must begin to measure relative to 100% with initial goals of 99.5% or better with an evolutionary path that shoots for 100%. Reaching that goal can mean several things like customer satisfaction, increased sales, reduced (if not eliminated) customer recovery costs and continued employment. All of these are very nice for the bottom line – especially the last one!

Now you change your view of numbers and instead of trying to convince anyone that you and your team are really busy and that you need more staff, you are now presenting why you are successful. And because of your metrics, your volumes have increased to support additional staffing once you increase your total output by employee.

Here is a service company that manages valves and widgets in the field. They get electronic notification of problems and must respond in a predetermined time frame. The customer also expects them to resolve the problems the same day – with exceptions permitted. That means they need to monitor the equipment (Hardware) in the field, the number of errors that the equipment generates electronically (Messages) and the problems documented and resolved by the engineer (Tickets).

Here's what you could look like:

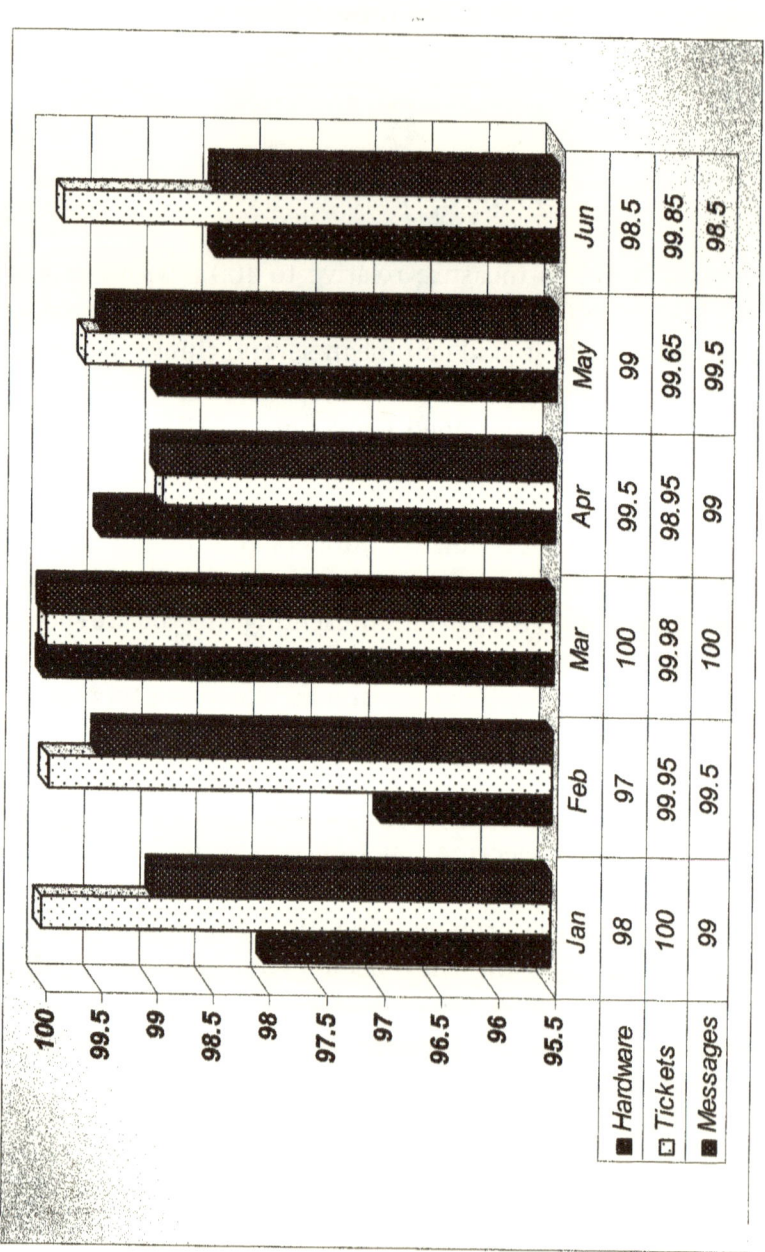

	Jan	Feb	Mar	Apr	May	Jun
Hardware	98	97	100	99.5	99	98.5
Tickets	100	99.95	99.98	98.95	99.65	99.85
Messages	99	99.5	100	99	99.5	98.5

According to this chart, you are meeting nearly 100% problem ticket resolution on the same business day and that's exceptional. Also, you are responding to equipment error messages within 2 minutes 98.5% of the time. Finally, your hardware was up 97% of the month of February, 98.7 % in April and 98.4% in June. So, let's look at the depth of each problem by comparing to service level agreements. Your SLA for tickets is 99.5% same day resolution. The SLA for equipment error response time is 98% within 2 minutes. And your hardware up time is 99%. Ooops – I think we see the obvious here.

What kind of message does this send? It sends one that highlights where your service level weakness really exists. But now you have a target to aim at that is focused on improvement and not blurred by volumes of statistics. Now you have **Metrics!** You may now focus on elevating your message response averages while you try to find out why your hardware up time has the consistency of bed springs. Both need to be addressed.

Once again, you had to turn the statistics around to view the depth of the issue and discover where the problem was instead of trying to convince your management that you can improve process by increasing head count. It just isn't true. Those who profess this fallacy have never been truly held accountable for their statement.

Granted, there are definitely times where head count will resolve an issue pointing strictly at increased volumes. But making mistakes is not a team issue it usually is a personal issue that results in a team effect. It is also one that can hurt visibility and destroy morale. You, as the manager, need to know when this is an issue and what you will have to do to address and eliminate the issue. But it usually cannot be done overnight and, once again, you cannot do it alone. You need the knowledge and support of your team. You need to have them educated on the source of the issue, knowledgeable of how it can and should be resolved and their overall commitment to making it happen.

Now, you can point at Hardware and Messages as two areas requiring improvement. I guarantee you that you can get their attention with these numbers because they report the frequency of failures and mistakes and not a commitment to volume.

I can recall working for a major bank and having a problem trying to get new hires on to our network so they can begin being productive. They could not even receive their e-mail until they were processed by our security team and added to the employee roster.

I called our security executive and stated that 5 days was not acceptable as we had contractors approved and on site in less than 3 days so we needed a system that could support our need. The response I received absolutely shocked me. "We process over five thousand of these requests every month"! Now what in blazes has that got to do with my question? Absolutely nothing! It was a response that was meant to impress me – it didn't. It was also an excuse – not a reasonable response indicating what could or should be done to support our need.

What I wanted was a change in service level. What I got was a statistical response focused on volume of work and not the proficiency in which it was being done. As a customer, I was not impressed.

Take every opportunity to re-earn your customer's support as an opportunity to extend their longevity as your customer. Don't try to impress your customers. Instead, let them be impressed at what you take for granted – extremely strong customer service but still seeking perfection.

So what do you want to invest your time in? Managing and reporting volumes or seeking perfection? I'm sorry to tell you this, but you have to do both. If you don't manage your volumes you have no measurement of activity relative to performance. If you don't manage performance you have no measurement of quality and the subsequent service you provide to your customer.

Both will take a good chunk of your time – or that of your staff. But make sure you share this responsibility with your staff as you are not the only person who needs to know about the level of service you provide and the quantity of work being performed. Your staff must be as well informed on this as you are. Besides, if the CEO casually talks with one of your direct reports, do you want them in a position of saying "Sorry I don't know?" or do you want them in a position to say "We offer our customer the highest service level available in our industry"!

Kind of warms your heart doesn't it – it's like a "thought hug"! That's where someone says something really nice about you, actually means it and smiles at you afterwards. Yes, it's your Mom but it still feels good doesn't it?

This section is probably the most difficult to get off the ground. It requires that you have a team of people who can relate to the stats and actually want to improve. Your greatest nemesis will be the one or two people who just don't get it. They think the entire process you have created is designed to get them out of their jobs so you can replace them. Every effort you present to assist you in explaining the process and objectives to them is met with fear, uncertainty and doubt (you know, *"FUD"*). No matter what you do, it appears that you will never get them to come over to the bright side, the positive side of quality improvement.

This is when the old expression of "fish or cut bait" may apply. By this time, you may have actually become fond of these people or this person but the cold hard fact still remains. That is, you may well have to let that person or those people go. It's chilling and seems callous but you have to draw the line. I have found that in almost every case, if I confronted the people or person with that very hard fact, they either begin the process of swinging over or they begin looking for another job.

Your objective here is to build a team and then show them how they look. Your statistics measures production volumes. Your metrics depict the quality of your team. If you do this right, both you and your team can be very proud of the achievements you reflect in your metrics.

Chapter Fourteen – Succession Planning & the Mack Truck Theory.

"Live life to the fullest. You never know when reality will force you into last place".

How many jobs are there "forever"? None! So why do you manage your job as if it will be there 30years from now so you can execute voluntary retirement and move to that two bedroom cottage in the mountains?

If you and your team are going to be successful today and tomorrow, you have to elevate your job to meet customer expectations while you remain competitive enough to retain your customer.

The best way to begin the process of elevation is by evaluating where you are today and start eliminating the activity that you no longer need to perform. By doing this, you can begin to assume the activities that are meaningful to your customers.

Figure "A"

Annual Job Review

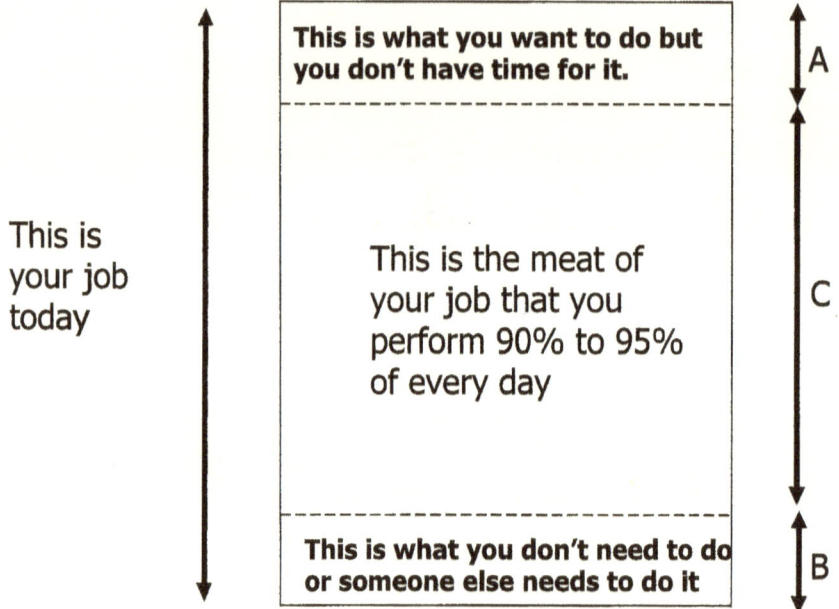

Eliminate "B" so you have time for "A"

The box in the diagram above has three layers of activity in it. The entire box represents what you are attempting to do today. As stated in each layer, the middle depicts around 80% of your normal business day. The bottom layer is what consumes 20% of your day and the top layer seldom gets done. Yet the most critical part of your job resides in this top layer.

What can you do to resolve this problem? Work with your manager and your staff and set this as a goal for all of you so that you can be more effective in your job role. Keep in mind that your staff has the same problem. The answer may be simple, complex or somewhere between the two – but there is an answer. I can guarantee you that the work you need to get rid of will probably consist of a large piece going to your direct reports. The balance may be something you just stop doing. And you have to be honest with yourself, your manager and your customers. Activity from your day may be reporting or statistical gathering that if something you were either told to do or have always done and it may be a perfect waste of your time.

Going back to figure (A), it is evident that this is a flat view with no depth. When you change a person's job role to exclude some activity and add others, chances are good that you are realigning the role to better reflect what is expected of the job role.

Figure "B"

Maintaining a Job

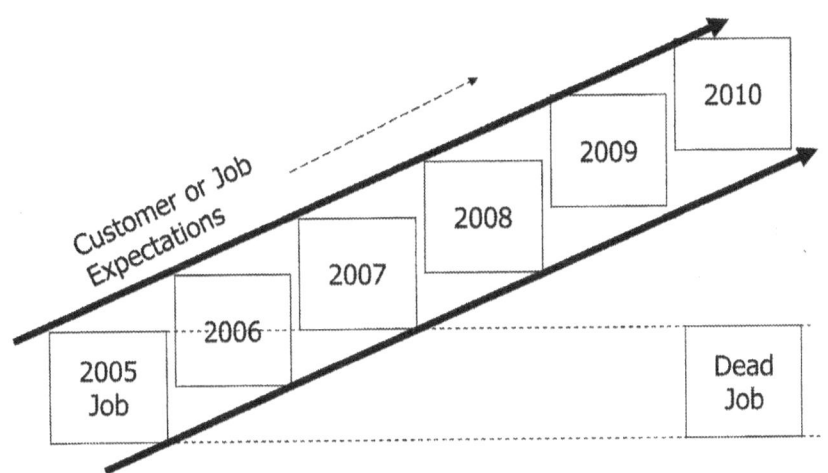

In 5 years, without elevating the job, it could be eliminated

With enough time and effort, you can see via Figure "B" that you can elevate a job to a new level whereby customer demand has eliminated the old job if it stays as it was, without change. That is definitely not good. However, this allows a job to continue existing and will have no impact on salary as it is merely meeting customer requirements.

Figure "C"

Elevating the Job

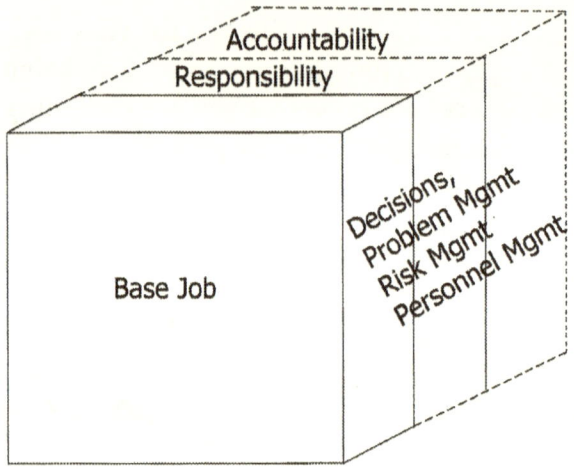

Adding Responsibility & Accountability increases the value of the job

However, when you increase a person's role to include more responsibility and subsequent accountability, you are now adding to their job role something that increases their value and subsequently their reimbursement. That's where the job description comes in. Now your effort needs to be focused on something near and dear to every employee – their job!

Figure "C" shows that you begin with a base job and by adding decisions, problem management, risk management and staff management – you add value. Because of that, you seriously increase the importance of the job. But, more important, you increase the responsibility and accountability of the job. And, if both those areas increase, the authorization that allows you to do your job is also added or increased.

Succession Planning

So what has this got to do with succession planning? Everything!

If you are going to evaluate your staff and identify who should be your successor, it has to be someone who is ready to assume your role today – not three years form now. And, if you have no one in a position to do that today, then you need to start building that potential ASAP! And where do you start? You do so by gradually assigning the person or people tasks that provide you with feedback on their current ability and their potential.

Years ago I was managing a data center and I had a staff to die for – they were intelligent, motivated and ready to assume additional work without hesitation. Of the people I had reporting to me; every one of them was capable of assuming my position with varying levels of success. Needless to say they were drawing lots on when the old guy would croak. Frankly I had died two years earlier and no one had the heart to tell me I was dead.

So, where does your staff rank? Since you are in the role, chances are good that the main reason you are in it is because none of them are capable – yet – of performing the job to an acceptable level. There lies your task. You need to determine how many of your staff can be trained to elevate to your role and by when.

There is a selfish reason for doing this you know. And it is because the chances of you moving up in your organization are based on how well you perform and how well you have trained your staff to succeed you. The left hand washes the right and your future promotions will be based on how well you manage your team and how well your manager prepared you for future growth.

If you want a good reference source – READ THIS BOOK! If you have your act together you will see that, through reading this book, you have work to do and time is of the essence. Here is what will help you build your team into an efficient machine with the capability to grow and allow you to move on to more of a challenge ....

You need to:

- Evaluate your staff to identify their strengths and weaknesses in their current job role and from that, you must determine what will make them ready for your job – and by when. If they can't manage their current role then chances are very slim that they can move up. Your assessment must consider how long it should take them to assume a more senior role and when you can begin to offload some of your work on to them to provide further assessment. From your evaluation of your staff, you must identify (1) who should go (2) who should grow and (3) who is your potential successor.

- Rank your staff in order of strengths. Who do you think is the strongest person on your staff today? Who can manage stress the best? Who is the best producer? Who is the strongest leader? Who gives the best sales presentations? Who is the most comfortable with management? Who has the respect of your team? This will allow you further food for thought. You want your staff to be happy so don't push anyone into a role you feel they should be seeking when they already are happy and want nothing more than to continue in that frame of mind.

- Who has the best education? Does he or she hold the best pen (or word processor)? Who has the best communications skills? Who is the most organized person? All of these assist in leadership roles but not necessarily your successor.

- Who caught your eye on Bill's team or Sarah's team? And I don't mean who is the best looking. It may be that the person whom you want to succeed you could be on someone else's team. If that's the case, you will need to go into overtime mode to prove that to your manager.

- Now that you have everyone ranked, what will you have to do to elevate any one of them to your role and how long will it take you to do it? The better you get at predicting and executing, the better you are at being a good manager.

Having a successor is actually something that intimidates many managers. They sometimes view it as a sign that when tough times come along you can be thought of as unnecessary. They feel they are at risk of being eliminated. They then become reluctant to assign additional responsibilities to their staff as it openly suggests they can do their manager's job. The employee is seldom given an opportunity to bring their ideas forward and present it to the manager's boss. Creativity is frozen and the chances of being successful with this manager are slim to none. Too bad! Everyone loses.

So what are you going to do differently? You are going to take a look at your job and break it into components that you will expose to your potential successors in the form of standard training (management 101). You must design succession training where you assign your potential successor(s) tasks that you currently perform. This allows you a means of determining how well they can do the job. And, when you are on vacation, you assign him or her, the task of doing it in your absence. It takes a great deal of trust to do that and a large amount of self confidence.

I'm impressed. You put your ego on hold and handed someone the opportunity to be you for a day or a week. That tells him or her a great deal about you and speaks volumes to your manager. Now look at the smile on the face of that employee. Notice how the smile on their face touches both of their ears? You did that!

OK, so now you're a pretty good manager. How do you become a great manager? You do it by being successful all the time – or at least most of the time. So don't stop at one – get as many as possible into the position of being your successor. You are not doing it to win the manager of the year award – you are doing it to assure a successor in your management slot. The successor could be in yet another department. Or it could be that you are creating great personnel in your own team. They may be happy as pigs in a barnyard in their current roles and all you did was make them even happier. There is nothing wrong with that.

Keep in mind that the intention is always to build your staff into the best employees that they can be. I don't believe you to be a loser if you built a staff that consists entirely of strong performers. That just makes you one heck of a strong manager.

Chapter Fifteen – Control – you will do it and you will love it!

"Every employee is a piece of clay waiting to be shaped – your job is to shape them, and then let them do what you trained them to do".

Back in the introduction I referenced "Empowerment". It was intended to point out the need to provide your staff with authorization to do their job. When anyone accepts a job, they usually have two things made very clear. Here is your job description and in it are your **responsibilities** and the associated activities for which you are also **accountable**. But seldom is anything mentioned about what you are **authorized** to do in order to resolve a problem. What is your signing authority? What can you order without your boss's permission? What can you approve so that you can delegate some of your responsibility?

There is nothing worse than being in a position to solve a problem but not have the authority to actually do it. So what are your alternatives? Do you do what needs to be done and beg forgiveness because begging permission takes three days and seven signatures? Do you run your legs off trying to find someone who does have authority – at two AM? Oh yes, and there is always the large government posture – do nothing and wait for all hell to break out so you can say, "I told you so".

Well, none of these options will leave the customer with words of thanks on their lips if your invested time yielded a result of you being fired, demoted or demoralized. The best plan is one that was prepared to give you control of a situation so you can identify the cause of the issue and make the necessary changes to resolve it and then prevent it from happening again.

When I think of "control" I think of that single stick coming up from the floorboard of a single engine aircraft. It's just you with the wind in your face and a one-ton aircraft 13,000 feet above sea level. You make a mistake and you pay it – assuming that the guy below you who took the afternoon off to cut the grass to please his wife isn't in direct line with your descent. But it is very simple. You have full control of your environment. You control your plane's take off through to its landing. You made all the calls and it was a successful venture.

Now put your manager in the co-pilot chair next to you. Make sure he has the power to grab the stick from your hands because he thinks you can't handle the demand of the role you are in. Put your brother-in-law in the back with the eject button to your seat. His only job is to evaluate the smoothness of the flight. Oh, and let your life partner manage the gasoline in your tank the day after you forgot their birthday. What kind of control do you have now?

Your staff is completely at your mercy when you prepare a task for them. Do you lead them and once they appear to have the pace, swing behind them and provide the support they need to get the job done at a high success rate? If not, you are back in that airplane.

So what can you do that will allow your team to perform at the highest possible level?

Trust them!

Aha – the "T" word. I know we already talked about this several times but it's more than worth the time to get into a bit more detail. How can you possibly trust someone that you barely know? You can't – so don't expect them to trust you just because you walked into a manager title. If you honestly believe you can lead a group without trust, you are sadly mistaken. Today's marketplace is yearning for employee loyalty but costs of benefits and mergers have made it impossible for employees to consider their company as their key loyalty. They have families that place huge demands on them and today's endless list of "I gotta have" items that place additional demands on the employee. The bottom line is income to offset expenses.

You know perfectly well that in order to build trust you have to prove yourself by setting expectations and meeting them. That's the key. Say you will do something and actually do it – what a fascinating concept! There's a gold star idea. I'm sure Six Sigma never thought of that!

So how do you build a plan that your team can execute? You start by slicing off a portion of the corporate goals and objectives and make it part of your team plans. You now have a piece of the corporate commitment that your team can understand, relate to and focus on as part of their annual objectives.

The plan you eventually put together has to include two sets of goals. Your goals and that of your team need to combine to form your ultimate objectives. Yours may be fairly simple – "Please the boss – do what he/she says". I would hope it is far more complex or your job boils down to nothing. Keep in mind that your goals are the group goals for your staff so make them achievable and measurable. They should be goals that can be dissected and distributed to your staff members. Then their goals become part of the overall goals and the ability to meet them becomes part of their performance review. See, it all comes together and the final proof is in the performance review.

Assuming you document those goals, the only thing left is to make sure that they are referenced regularly so no one forgets why they were documented. The fact that the corporate goals have become part of each person's final review means that the goals are in fact a living document and everyone in the organization is part of the success and growth of the organization.

Many companies will use the bonus program to support the objectives. The employee is financially rewarded for meeting or exceeding the goals. There is no doubt in my mind that an employee has to have goals and objectives that reflect the corporate goals and objectives. This makes them more in tune with why the company is doing well or poorly and allows them to feel the commitment needed to drive them and thus make the company more successful.

Faith First

It is truly difficult building faith in anyone that you have not known a considerable length of time. Your childhood friends remained that way because you evolved together in almost anything you did. Sports, dating, zits, trying vices and doing all the things your parents told you not to do. You did it together and the most important element is that you backed each other up when things got a little rough. So how do you compare that to the way you manage?

Unless you feel that one of your reports is one of Satan's first born, you will have to extend a little faith to them and state that it is now their responsibility to perform certain tasks. The trick is to make certain that you will not question their ability to perform those tasks. Yet, the second you let those words out of your mouth you feel you should perform a recall and go back to your office. However, it is imperative that they know you are supporting them. So, you do what you know you have to do – you extend a fraction of your trust to them to see if they use it or abuse it. And, if they fail, and you know it was a result of anything but lack of effort. Because of that, you allow them to retain that trust as everything can be resolved through training & education. Effort is something they either have or do not have. You cannot substitute it. Effort grows with the ability to be held accountable as long as they feel they have the authorization they need in order to perform the task.

Each time you extend more faith into their side of the room, you are in fact building that trust. And, if you know you can trust that person to do the job the way it needs to be done, then you are fully prepared to support them no matter what the issue or the cause.

So what is your level of trust? Are you yet in that position to stand on your desk and with your arms folded at the chest, remaining vertical and fall backwards in their general direction? No way! They have not yet proven to you that they can react to all the problems that can occur in your line of work and resolve the problems without severe customer impact. And you have not proven that you can lead them through it.

The career test!

This problem occurs against all the odds and it has no recovery plan. It is when all hell breaks out and you have to fall back on the expertise of each individual on your team. You will have to rely on their drive and their commitment to their job and the company to see all of you through the recovery process until it has been healed. Whether it is the near loss of a key account, a server failure that has no backup or anything else you place in the category of hellacious. It is the time when you need them the most and you hope to discover that you can trust them to "get the job done".

Yes indeed, your entire body puckers until the word comes out that everything was recovered and the cause was outside your control. You exhale for about 15 minutes and reconsider that job in Montana managing a herd of llamas. You then realize that Bob, Sally, Jeff and Sue just saved your career by doing what they do best and they did it out of reaction and without you standing over them saying "How much longer", "Is it done yet", "Do you have any idea how bad this will look if you don't recover from this"?

This is the time that you feel liberated from demand because you know you have someone on staff that can carry the ball when you need them to do so and probably will be your successor. It's a great feeling until they come to you a week later with their request for a serious salary increase or – worse yet - a letter of resignation. Yes, it can blow a huge hole in your sails to experience a loss so soon after an amazing save but you already know that you have to stay on top of these potential issues. If you do not, you have only yourself to blame.

Recognition of Effort

The last step to winning over your staff is to properly reward them for their efforts. It does not have to be a certified check for thousands of dollars, although it definitely would not hurt. What people want from you is equal portions of respect, patience, understanding and consideration. No more – no less. A fair reaction for each and every action is always warranted. A little praise, some casual recognition and during those exceptional moments, a group reward of elevated visibility.

If your budget – or your personal funding – allows the next step, please submit them to some tangible rewards. A gift certificate, a dinner for two and the ever appreciated check are a great addition to the casual "Attaboy or Attagirl". But don't get hung up on the tangible side of rewarding your staff. I have had well reimbursed people come to me and ask why I don't spread more kudos to the team. They are not after the tangibles that many managers think is required to satisfy their need for recognition of effort. They merely want to know that someone is watching them and that their efforts are visible and appreciated.

Getting people to "get the job done" is not a stand alone task. It is a bag full of requirements that are owned in part by everyone on the team. But it is the manager who is responsible for putting all the pieces together and making sure they fit. One piece out of place and you end up with a dysfunctional team.

You know you have control over any situation when your team has that same sense of control. They are responsive, tactical and analytical. They look for problems, anticipate the inevitable and plan for the potential of even worse. They take the time to look into problems so they can eliminate them, not patch them up. And, without any involvement from you, they follow up to make certain what they attempted to do was in fact achieved.

All of the aforementioned is based on whether your team has already been walked through the fundamental need of the four questions you ask for a Root Cause Analysis - by you or your predecessor.

The only thing more beautiful than a team of well groomed horses is watching them move along in perfect timing, proud of their job and happy to be where they are at that time. I am not attempting to compare any team of people to a team of horses but rather the precision with which they work. It isn't important whether you brought that to the team or it was already there and in use. The important part is that it exists and is being used.

Let's see. You have provided your team with a direction, and you have given the initial trust (where you can) as well as the authorization to back you up. You are attempting to provide a form of reward where possible and you are making certain that their efforts are visible to your management.

With that said, you have reached a point where you can trust your team to do the job they are trained to perform and you can go home and sleep tonight.

Chapter Sixteen – Working like a team!

"I never felt that I was anything less than a member of a team – even when I was working by myself".

Just how over worked is that cliché – "Working like a team"?

I cannot remember anyone resorting to a different phrase when attempting to motivate me or the group of people I was included with at the time of the presentation or oration. They were making every effort to make us see as one – perform as one – relate as one. There is no "I" in team! Goals are achieved through teamwork and destroyed by individualism and closed minds.

I hate to say this, but it is indeed true.

Today, there are dozens of "Right Ways" to do things and there are a number of documented procedures to follow that allow you to improve efficiency and quality by reducing errors and repeating correct processes. ISO 9000, 17799, 19011 and Six Sigma and many others were created to allow you a means of identifying and correcting processes that are inefficient, incorrect or improperly implemented. You then design and implement a process that can be repeated with recurring efficiency and with success. You end up creating a successful, repeatable process.

So what about the people? How do you get a hodge-podge of people to think and act as one? First of all, is it even attainable? What is the probability of having a crew of people gel and begin working as a single cohesive unit? Before I realized I was a change insurgent, I would have suspected it is very low. But now I know better.

Literally everyone wants to be part of a successful team. Yes, they want individual recognition from their management, their peers and their customers. But they also want to be part of something that is greater than the sum of its parts. They want to be challenged and subsequently rewarded for their effort and above all, they want to be seen as being an integral part of a team of people. So how do you motivate each person to move to the middle of the room and become part of a department that is currently dysfunctional? You don't. You motivate them to be a contributor at an individual level and then you educate them on how they can exceed their personal expectations by sharing and trusting a group of people they know little or nothing about.

This is where you come in! You are the glue that holds all the pieces together initially because you have to take the time to see how all of your staff (pieces) fit together and what changes you and they will have to make to allow them to work as one team. But after a period of time (it may or may not be determined by you) the melding process needs to take place and they become the unit of one and you become the guidance system.

I stated some time ago that you have to know when to stand in front of your team and when to stand behind them. Both require perfect timing and neither one is clearly definable as to exactly when you should do it. But, in time, you will know.

You have to know when to step in front to provide protection, guidance, support and overall leadership. Then, when rewards and kudos are being awarded, stand back and behind your team so they can feel the warmth of recognition. They need to see both of these from the time you walk into your new role. You will then see the results of your effort – not necessarily as quickly as you might like, but you'll see the results when you really need to. It will most likely appear at a time of mild or severe crisis.

Get Control Quickly

You have already evaluated your team so you know who the keepers are and who needs to be approached for some corrective guidance. Be direct, be fair and be quick. You don't have a silver bullet for group recovery so your team has to know if they are going to require some surgery. I have yet to walk into an organization that required nothing more than some solid direction and a manager they could trust and respect. Granted, I have had to release some people who were too far gone. By that I mean they were so fed up with previous management that they could no longer remember what success looked like and they were incapable to being redirected. Too bad, they were probably walking assets until bad management turned them against everything.

Find your leader. This is the person who is most respected by the team and capable of leading them when you cannot. You may also find that this person is potentially one of your successors. But don't be offended if the person states that they don't want anything to do with management. I have seen many times where a strong technical leader needs to stay there for a very long time before they want to see something different. They are personally rewarded by their hands on environment. You take that away from them and it's kind of like taking sunlight away from a flower. They fade quickly.

Now you need to look at all the strengths of each player and make certain they too are in the right job. Your most creative need to design and build while your anal retentive need to test and structure procedures. Your high energy personnel need to perform quality review and change control. And last, but certainly not least, your middle of the road need to perform reiterative functions, follow procedures and perform their creativity in a more contained environment.

Now you have what you need, it's time to mould them into a team.

There are plenty of manuals and books out there that are entirely focused on team building. Once again, let the people with the real answers provide you with the knowledge base you need to logically build a team. All I can offer you as reference are the experiences I have had in building them and keeping them running. It's not easy.

It helps to have a major project to reference as you focus your team on the goals. That alone can provide a reference point and a series of stepped objectives that serve as individual and team objectives that can be measured. If you don't have one – create one. It needs to be something that your manager can approve and it has to yield a goal that they believe in as individuals. Re-writing their job descriptions is a great source of individual assignments that relate to the person while the team focuses on properly documenting what is expected of their unique job roles. If their jobs have not been reviewed in the last 2-3 years, then they are due. Plus, they may benefit financially if the jobs are upgraded. But don't bet on it. Just when you least expect it, the jobs can be down graded too. Make absolutely certain that you do a class "A" job on assessing, defining and documenting the jobs, the risks associated with the jobs and the skills required to perform them.

Get Buy-in

Assuming you have defined goals and objectives for each person and the team, you now need their undivided attention so you can determine if you are going to get the support you need. There's nothing worse than leading a charge and just as you enter the kill zone you look over your shoulder to see that no one is behind you. It kind of gives new meaning to the word *"dork"*.

If you cannot sell your staff on what you intend to accomplish in the next year, pack your bags and go home because you haven't a snowball's chance in hell in accomplishing a reasonable percentage of success let alone the entire plate of objectives. You have to have all of them on your side – or at least thinking that way – before you can consider taking the first step. The best way to handle this is to assure you have a full understanding of what each person wants to achieve and an even better understanding of what they need in order to be successful.

Going back to those all important one-on-one sessions, refer to your notes. Find out what each person needs and see if you can provide it without giving up the crown jewels. I bet that the most they would want is a salary review and some respect. Both of those are inside your control.

If you believe you know what the objectives are and you also believe **IN** those objectives, you can sell them to your team. Your people are not dummies but they are not robots either. Make certain you can convey the message in a clear and simple format that includes your energy and enthusiasm. Both have to be real and honest or you may as well take that energy and try swimming the English Channel because you will have a better chance at that than convincing your team that you are worth following.

OK – you convinced them to follow you, you have enticed them to commit their energy towards the objectives that you have defined and thanks to the effort you put into the description of the projects you are having them working on, you now have their buy-in.

So, what's next?

Communication – communication – communication!

This part is the easiest – let them take control while you guide them and make certain you update them daily (or at least on a defined regular basis) on the management view of the successes thus far. By doing this, they can update you daily on their progress relative to the timeline and objectives. In other words – you communicate with them and they communicate with you. It is so very easy yet many leaders of major projects under communicate the success and progress only to over communicate the failures. It's kind of like that old adage "The beatings will continue until morale improves". Too many managers feel that their people are motivated by fear and live by uncertainty and doubt.

No one needs that kind of life.

Keep your team abreast of the action. Let them know everything that is going on with the budget, the relative success, the timeline and the percentage complete. Communicate executive opinion – good or bad. Any news is better than no news. And, let other people know of your overall progress. Good news travels very fast – especially if you tell one of your peers or the peers of your staff. All news makes it back to your team – but nothing travels faster than bad news or a condescending statement. If you want to demoralize your team in less than 60 seconds, make a shallow off hand remark about your team to an associate in a rest room.

Review

Let's see what we have here. We have a new manager with a new group of people that he or she wants to shape into a new team. That manager has taken the time to meet and understand each of the direct reports to get a better understanding of where they are, where they want to be and what they believe it takes to be successful. That same manager has acted swiftly in forming the team, educating the doubters and removing the incapable. Last, and by all means certainly not least, that very same manager made a commitment to each team member that he or she would communicate everything to them and not hold back the bad or the really good.

So we now have a body of people marching towards a common goal, lead a person they believe they can trust with a documented objective and a work environment based on listening and communicating.

Sounds like a winner to me!

Chapter Seventeen – Budget Planning – understanding it and making it work!

"BUDGET – is Latin for Tight Wad".

This has to be the most challenging area you will have to learn and manage of all the tasks assigned to a manager. It is a thankless job that requires you manage a sometimes predetermined amount of money (like salary increases that are held to a fixed percentage) and allocate it to a body of people where everyone feels they are exceptional performers.

Capital and Expense

There are several related areas that define the budget for your team. However, they all boil down to one of two cost allocations -Capital and Expense. Capital is anything that is purchased by you or your team that costs over a predetermined amount. For example, it may be the position of your Accounting Department that anything over $500 is viewed to be an asset. Depending on the company, a common rule is that if it is over $500 and it has a life of three years you must depreciate it over 3 years, no more. Personal computers, again depending on the company, will be depreciated over a three to five year plan. That means that, if a PC costs $500, your budget will be charged a recurring expense of $100 a year for the next 5 years.

Keep in mind that if your budget is approved, anything you purchase as an asset will sit in your budget as a recurring expense for the next 3-5 years. Therefore, if your budget is flat lined (no increase from year to year), your expense allocation gets smaller as your annual depreciation expense increases. Therefore, watch your spending on assets. If you can release an asset even if it is not fully depreciated, you may want to look into the costs you would incur to perform an early release. This applies if the asset is broken or no longer performing the function you purchased it to perform. However, if it involves an early write off, that too comes out of your budget.

Here's another factor. Whether you purchase or lease equipment, the federal, state and local government will levy a property tax on that equipment as long as it resides in that county. If you move to another county, then the tax travels with it to that new location. This is usually not part of your immediate budget but I guarantee you that it will eventually make its way back to your budget – so plan for it too.

Here's a hypothetical budget scenario. You buy a good PC that is expected to last 5 years. You spend $750 on it so your budget is hit with a depreciation of $150 a year for 5 years. You also purchase a $300 printer that is expected to last 3 years so it is amortized (proportionately split over the three years) at $100 a year. You forecast that in 2008 you will buy a new desk and get rid of your orange crate. The desk will cost $2,000 and will be amortized over 10 years so you have another $200 applied to your depreciation schedule for 2008 for the next 10 years.

For now, forget about the thousands of dollars in your budget and let's just look at a budget of three items. In 2006 you have an annual expense of $250 (PC and printer depreciation). In 2007, you continue your annual depreciation of the PC and the printer for $250. In 2008, you pick up a desk and that adds another $200 a year to your expenses. In 2009, the printer has been fully depreciated so you have only the PC and desk expense that year of $450. And then in 2010, your PC is fully depreciated and your annual costs drop to only $200 a year.

Here's a picture of what just a few assets can do to your bottom line:

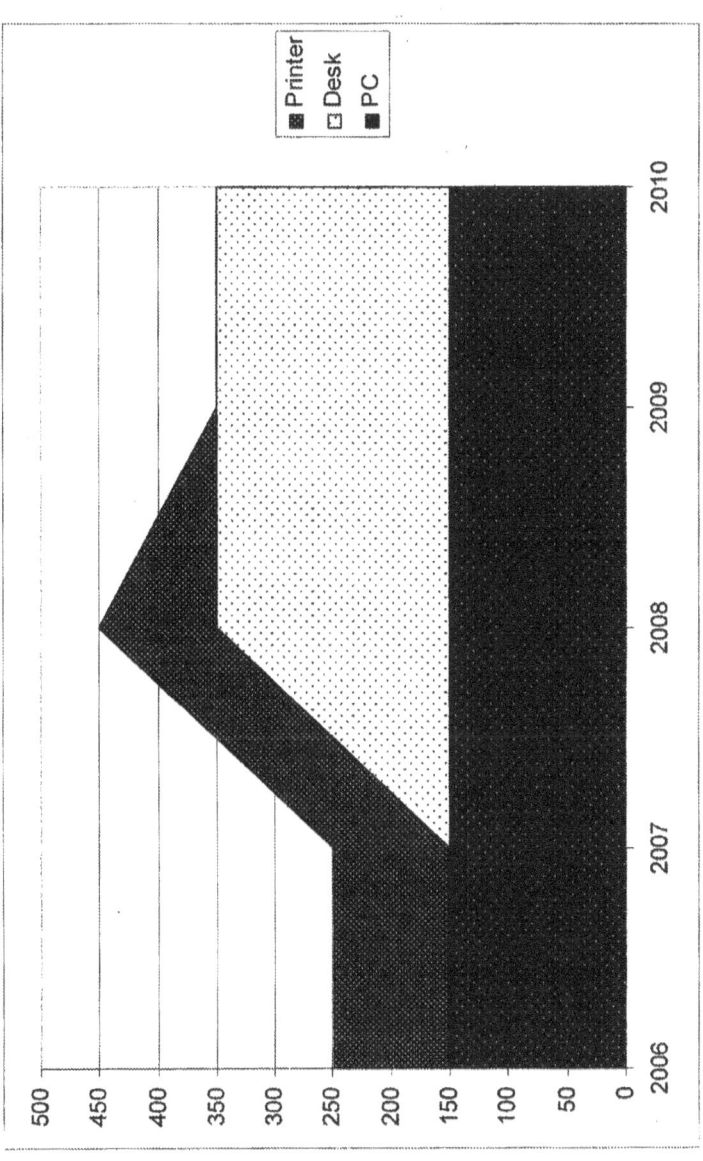

Expenses

Your budget must include every expense item that you and your team incur as a result of the business function you perform. Here is a hit list of items that are usually included in your departmental expenses.

- Telephone expenses – includes all expenses for your telephone system, monthly line rentals, fax lines, voice lines, data lines, voice mail and internet or cable services.
- Utilities are usually charged back from the facilities group as part of your costs for square footage and building services (garbage collection, security, cleaning, etc.). You'll just see one line item – facilities.
- Travel & entertainment – this includes meals, hotel, rental car and air flights
- Training & education – including seminars and vendor shows and also including reimbursed education for degree programs and technical training
- Contract services – includes temporary help, vendor services excluding anything associated with development costs which can be capitalized.
- Salary and benefits – for full time and part time employees and temporary assistance.
- Postage and mailing – courier services included.
- Miscellaneous expenses – anything that does not fall into one of the previous categories

Budget Surprises

Ever heard of the $150,000 dumb terminal? Well I personally experienced the purchase of one.

This is something I saw happen when managing a data center in Canada in the very early 1980's. In those days, there were only dumb terminals available to view something on a mainframe from a remote location – no PC's were affordable at that time as they went for over $10,000 per unit. Every department would budget their terminal and printer costs every year and each request went through my team for acquisition, order and install.

One of the divisions ordered a new terminal. Now, each one of those terminals was connected to what was known as an IBM communications controller called a model 3174. Each of these 3174's could manage up to 32 devices – printers or terminals. With minimal research we determined that the $1,200 terminal would require a new controller as the one in their area was now full. A controller cost around $24,000. This was not unusual so we placed the unit on order and charged back one twenty-fourth the cost to that same department. The terminal was now going to cost them $2,200 plus installation and the project costs were now at $25,200.

Our technical analyst came back to me that afternoon with a smirk on his face commenting that we had another surprise. The 3174 remote controller connected via coaxial lines to an expansion port on the mainframe. In order to connect a controller it needed to attach via a communications card inside the mainframe. You guessed it, the card was maxed out and we had to order another one. Then to add insult to injury, we were advised that the expansion chassis was attached via channel cable and the mainframe had no more expansion ports – we had to upgrade the mainframe.

By the time the smoke cleared on this project, the project cost was up to **$150,000** without installation costs. Needless to say, when the line of business manager was told his dumb terminal would cost over $150,000 he was certain we were attempting to pull his leg. Then, when he realized we were serious, he set a new record for the highest pitch squeal emitted by a human being before imploding.

Well, thanks to the courage of our IT Director, we ordered the equipment and absorbed the majority of the costs (and charged back as the new users were added) so that the department head only saw an invoice for $1,200. The lesson learned here was to stay very much ahead of the curve in planning. No matter what happened that year, we were going to run out of space on our mainframe and had it been planned ahead of time, it would have been upgraded prior to the demand. Then, it would have been clearly visible to our management that we would incur this expense.

Head Count

I saved this heading for last as a commemoration to one of my favorite people. This lady was a fireball with a love for detail and instant recall. But she had a heck of a time trying to figure out head count. Head count is quite basic but proved to be exceptionally challenging for her.

Every year you have a given head count that was approved as part of your budget. For example, you may have eight people reporting to you plus your position. Therefore you have a department head count of nine. If someone resigns or transfers or is promoted to a position outside of your area, you still have the head count, it's just not fully occupied with people. Therefore you have nine positions with only eight filled. That means you have one unfilled position. Your head count remains the same, but you have to report (monthly or by quarter) where you are relative to where you need to be. This is where she got confused and wanted to know if she reported eight heads or nine because there were logically only 8 heads since one of the heads left. I had to get a little creative.

To help her, I used an analogy of buckets and strawberries. Each approved position you have in your department is a bucket. Your management has approved you to have 8 positions plus your own. – whether or not a person occupies that role. When you hire someone (a strawberry) you now place that person into that bucket – which is a job role or position. With one person leaving, you then have eight strawberries and nine buckets.

The bottom line is that you need to protect your staff or strawberries, but you really have to work much harder to protect your buckets or head counts. But not nearly as much as you have to protect your posterior when head count reduction takes place.

I hope this little analogy assisted in providing you a better description of the relationship between a head count and the person occupying the associated job role. It should also allow you to see the reasoning behind why you need to fully understand the relationship. The last thing you can allow yourself to do is to **not know** your head count when your manager asks you for it. If you don't the next reduction could well be your own head.

Your Budget

The bottom line is always your responsibility. In this case it is how well you define and project your needs and that of your staff in capital, expense and head count. You only get one shot at it and there is no room for error. If you fall short of your forecast, you had better have a very close rapport with your boss because he or she will have to cover your assets when ever you fall short.

Focus on 12 consecutive months, the needs your team has and what you need so they can "get their job done". Your intentions should be to prepare a budget that does not significantly exceed last year's budget (try to stay within the salary increase range of around 2%). Make certain any increase is explainable and provides a return on investment.

Once again, your objective is not to have a larger budget than any of your peers. That is flat out suicidal. Instead, you are trying to layout a financial plan to meet the objectives assigned to you by your manager, your customers and your staff. You are going to acquire the tools that make a difference in your service level. You are also going to educate your staff so that the customer enjoys working with them. And, you are going to continue to invest in technology that allows you to see problems before they happen. The net effect is unquestionable service for a well defined customer.

Your budget is your lifeline to good management. You need to be absolutely certain that the forecast you put together on it is extremely accurate (within reason). It must be reflective of your goals and objectives and can be justified from start to finish. This is one case where it is **VERY** important to be right!

Chapter Eighteen - Bringing it all together – you can't do it alone!

"I've never failed! However, some of my successes have been extremely limited".

What a handful you have now! You have taken on a new role that requires you grow faster than you ever have before. You need to quickly gain the respect of your staff, your peers and your customers. There are many problems to resolve and many more that you will address as you resolve others. Your learning mechanism is in full throttle and your nerves are being tested every day. So how do you plan to bring everything together?

If you have convinced yourself you can do it on your own, repeat after me **"I am a bonehead, I am a bonehead, I am a bonehead".**

I do believe you've got it! You have officially accepted that you can't do everything yourself and you will have to fall back on periodic assistance from your boss, your staff and your peers. Your boss can help you sort out the customer relationships, project priority and budget issues. Your staff can help you deal with the day to day demands of your customers and business unit counterparts. Your peers can introduce you to their teams, several other peers outside of your department and vendors whom you have yet to deal with.

All of this will be of mammoth assistance so you can focus on learning and changing.

The actual act of getting it all together will be primarily the execution of a plan that you put together in the first 30 days of employment in your new role. No more and definitely no less. If you can't get the basics together in the first two weeks you were not meant to be in the role you now have. The next two weeks are entirely for preparing a 60,000 foot plan of how you will strategize your next year.

Surprised? You shouldn't be! The demands of your creative mind in the first 30 days will be exceptional. What you have to learn is indeed of great substance. But what you must plan is even more demanding.

Remember when I stated that you may be lucky and only have to worry about screwing up a great group of people? Well, chances are very good – and not in your favor – that there is no possibility at all that you will enjoy that luxury. Every group has its dysfunctional members, failing projects, budget challenges and misdirected goals and objectives. I assure you, yours will be no exception.

This is where your manager plays his or her greatest role. They must provide you with the information you don't have the time to discover. Actually, it will probably be on paper for you in the form of task assignments that your manager wants you to address first. Even if they are broad and generic, they are key starting points for you to address.

For example, you may have the following list of requirements from your manager:

1. Turn around the Farbroker project – it is three months behind, $400,000 over budget and the business unit wants to pull your group off the project. (This is like finding out

your check for your down payment on your first apartment just bounced – and you moved in yesterday).

2. Look into allegations that Joseph, your best accountant, is dipping into corporate funds with false expense account entries. (He's the big guy with a face that is so red it looks like his head is going to explode).

3. Look into out sourcing some of your responsibilities to reduce cost and avoid head count increases. (Your team knows about this and all but one circulated their resumes last week because each of them thinks his or her job is being eliminated).

4. Start planning a relocation of your team to the downtown office so you can be closer to the business units. (It's 15 miles further for you to commute and the one person who is not job searching lives two buildings away from the new location)

Isn't life great?

Now you have to make a series of decisions on how you are going to prioritize and plan each of these requirements. You also need to determine how many of them are your tasks, what goes on the back burner and what your boss and staff can do for you. I told you that you couldn't do this on your own!

Planning and executing have to be your two strongest skill sets. Neither of them requires previous management experience. They are the result of a well organized mind and total lack of fear in taking on a challenge. You have a number of other traits that made you a great fit for the manager role but these two are your bread and butter strong business sense characteristics.

Here is the best advise I can give you for a time like this:

162 — *Ray Labadie*

Take them one at a time!!

There is no way that you can execute on all of these at the same time but you can allocate your time – and that of your staff – to each one so they are all being addressed in parallel with one another. Hopefully, you already know who your "Go To" person is as he or she will be your right hand while you sort out these issues. But first – you have to prioritize everything.

Although there are four key issues, you still have lots of other activities to keep you busy. But your highest attention level needs to be on the four key issues. Take a surface look at each one of your tasks. The Farbroker project is important but you will need to spend some solid time on it along with the person you have that is leading the project. I'd suggest setting up time tomorrow with the project leader, Bill, to see if he has been smoking some imported substance rather than focusing on the project. Then meet with your boss and ask for some support in preparing a project review and a meeting of the minds with the line of business.

Joseph wins! Anything that hints of financial misdoings could easily appear on your Sarbanes-Oxley report (aka SOX) and the name after it could easily be yours. Get to this one right away.

Wait a minute, out sourcing is always a concern but first you need to deal with your staff. Yes, you have a relocation plan to put together but if you don't have any staff you could be relocating air. This is an ultra number one project. No staff on hand makes it real easy to cancel a project that is falling behind. But, do you want to be the one that walks into a meeting to declare you have just lost key staff members and your project is taking a hike?

Go to work on your staff and show them that their jobs are in place and just fine and that the focus of the project is on preventing head count add by strategically out sourcing. Then prove it to your boss.

With that out of the way, go to your best staff member with a gift for design and layout. Let him or her propose your space requirements – especially if that person has worked for several years in your department. That kind of history is invaluable for strategically planning space for the next 3-5 years.

Now you can focus on the financial accusations on Joseph. This is the best time to seek out your financial peer and see what that department can do for you. It could simply be a clear cut case of someone falling into the valley of assumption with the real fault being sloppy reporting. You can only hope. But the best way to address this issue is with an open mind and a very smart accounting person to help you. Once you have gathered all the facts, you then need to sit with Joseph and find out if he has a personal goal of owning an island in the Mediterranean or if he spends all his weekend in Atlantic City.

Good for you!

You jumped into the river of demand and swam across it and back. You made full use of your resources – your boss, your staff and your peers. You sought out the best performers and gave them plenty of direction and freedom. You made them accountable for the completion of the tasks and directed them to report findings and output back to you. And at no time did your hands leave your wrists.

Impressive.

Could you have done this without reading this section? Probably! If you are:

- Self motivated enough to assume responsibility for tasks assigned to you
- Disciplined enough to sort out your issues by priority
- Flexible enough to trust your staff and open enough to seek you manager's assistance,

Then, chances are very good you were going to execute as required. If the answer to any of the aforementioned was "sort of" or "kinda", then maybe a little advice was warranted.

The good news is that at the end of one very busy week you will probably find out the following:

1. The Farbroker project was behind because of the business unit constantly changing their minds and executing the most critical of all project sins – **Scope Creep.** This is where they insist that the project was supposed to include any number of things that would make their life easier and yours far more complicated. Bill was not smoking anything but rather trying to put out the fires caused by an uncaring business unit that was seeking to pressure your team into committing to goals that would have caused the project to over run into the millions.

2. Joseph is clean. He was submitting expense account claims for mileage using his odometer reading that were in kilometers – not miles. Since part of his job is to drive to each business location and retrieve backup disks for off site storage, he puts about 30 miles on his car every day. What he didn't know was that his Pontiac had a toggle switch that his four year old played with and showed 50 instead of 30. Certainly not worth firing over but did force a review of all of his expense accounts for the last year.

3. Outsourcing is always a tough topic to manage. But in this case, you found a way to prevent hiring another analyst by reallocating work and eliminating activities that were no longer required. And, you formed a review sequence that allowed your staff to look at this every quarter to see if work that they can never seem to get to should be outsourced.

4. You and your staff are now relocated and your office area pleases everyone. You can now share AA support with your peer in Marketing which reduced cost and square footage so now even your boss is happy.

I told you that you couldn't do it alone!

I have seen many of my friends and peers nearly destroy themselves trying to assume control of everything without anyone's help. It's a crying shame. They burn themselves out and no one is ever the wiser – especially that person that is burned out.

Recently I told one of my peers the very same thing but he was open to my opinion and immediately went to work delegating activity on his team. He shocked many of his staff because he had gotten to the point where they were performing mundane tasks and suddenly he was actually giving them serious assignments. That will draw a toothy smile out of the Mona Lisa.

Doing this once doesn't mean you can check the box marked "organized" and never see it again. It needs to be a daily activity. You have just created a habit that is infectious – and you don't have to take any medication either. It's a good habit and one that will continue to reward you as long as you maintain its constant use.

Good luck!

Chapter 19: Anger Management

"If I could just get him to calm down, I'd loosen my grip on his throat".

There's no doubt about it – anger management is the topic du jour and has been for the last decade. Road rage and domestic violence have reached an apex in media exposure and it looks as though day time talk shows are still making big money exposing us in our worst moments. So how do we manage ourselves in such a way that we can provide our team with good management without having to appear as the leading role on a 3 minute television special? Frankly, it is entirely within your control.

You need to look back a short while ago and evaluate your management in the last few years. Which ones stand out in your mind? The very best manager you had and the very worst? That makes sense. But what do you remember most about both? Once again, it is all too easy. The very best manager handled your mistakes and your successes the same way. By using them as pointers to growth opportunities!

You made a mistake and with the patience of Zen, he or she walked you through the process so you could better relate to the incidents that transpired. Then your manager allowed you to highlight the moment where you could have made a positive difference but made a poor choice and subsequently one or more people paid the price for your mistake. One of them was probably you! Because they chose to do that, you learned a valuable lesson and probably never made that mistake again.

Now, let's look at your worst manager. He crawled up one side of you and down the other voicing out loud what most people keep under their breath. He fell back on every other mistake you have made since birth and blamed at least one of the world wars on you. After spraying most of his words on your shirt, he now sits back with a pulse of 277 and attempts to get some color in his face, other than pure red. You now feel eleven inches high – at best – and you have no idea how many other people heard it as well. Your greatest decision now is whether to crawl out of his office or take on a full sprint. It was certainly not a proud moment for you. How is it that I know? Once again, easy – because I had it happen to me all too many times. Sadly enough, I did it to my staff as well. I am not proud of having done that. Granted, I learned a valuable lesson but I lost the respect of the person I chewed out.

There is far too much at stake when you lose the respect of a direct report – or a peer – or anyone for that matter. It could be that the person you treated like dirt under your shoe may some day be in a position to help you and chose not to at a critical point in your career. Worse yet, you lost an opportunity to create a lifetime friend or associate just because you chose to prove yourself right.

So, just how important is it to be right?

Heat of the Moment

If I reflect back to when I had my best opportunity to elevate myself and chose to shoot myself in the foot, it was when I had the most work related pressure on me. It is during those times that you have the least amount of time and patience and yet it should be a time when you are prepared to invest the most time and patience in your staff. It will probably be the most demanding time in your management career and will be a true test of just how far you will go as a manager.

But are you aware of just how well – or poorly – you are managing the demands and pressures of your job? Chances are very good that you will be the last one to know that you are a walking lunatic. You will probably think that you are an effective manager and unless you have a very close rapport with your staff and peers, you will continue thinking that when the truth is much further away.

I have personally experienced this during a peak pressure time and was fortunate enough to have a direct report tell me that I had my head in the sand. Thank goodness I was capable of listening to that person and prepared to hear what was said.

I have watched business associates self destruct and have absolutely no idea what was happening to them. I an uncertain if they were just too far gone or if they were incapable of hearing what others were trying to tell them. Either way, they chose not to take the advice of others and continued to abuse their staff and eventually were dismissed.

If you reach that point in your career or if you have someone you trust come to you and offer some free advice, take it and hold it in front of you so you can really see the cause and effect of your attitude. Your next step will be the most critical. Get help! If your company offers and employee assistance program, then use it and get on the phone and contact them. They can help. They can refer you to a field specialist who can help you relax and see where you should be versus where you are.

Assuming you sought and found some assistance, you will see in a very short time frame that you have more time and you are a far better listener. Very soon afterwards you will notice a change in your attitude – and so will your staff. You will handle stress far better and you will also see the other side of the problem. It will all occur because you can now wait to listen for an explanation. Even if it was a lousy explanation, you can tell the person that and make them go back and provide the real truth to the situation. You will have the patience to hear out the explanation and will actually hear yourself saying "I've been there and felt the same way" without looking for something to throw.

All of a sudden, you have some patience!

Now, it is no longer a matter of what this person did *to you*; it is merely what this person did. The weight of the world will no longer be on you and problems will have no where near the magnitude they did just a few short months ago. You can handle it. You will be able to hear out the problem **and** the explanation. Even if the explanation is less believable than the stories associated with Area 51.

Watch yourself!

Before you get too far into your management career, make certain that you can control your reaction to problem scenarios and remain focused. If you can handle the heat of a serious problem that was created by a staff member – without blowing up – then you are where you need to be. However, the real test is in how you manage the employee after the problem is resolved. You have an opportunity to be one of the glowing memories in the life of your employee – or the black hole of grief. The option is yours! Just remember, the grief you cause will quite possibly create a significant emotional experience for that employee that he or she may never overcome. It isn't a matter of what weight you can carry for the rest of your life; it is a matter of what they have to carry based on the words you chose to use to describe them as an employee – in your eyes.

Think back to the most recent failure you experienced. Was there a best friend or family member close by to help you through the emotional experience? And what was your manager like? Did he or she address it in such a way that you maintained your self respect? Did your manager choose to use you and your experience as a reference subject in your next staff meeting?

If you are to assume the role of manager, you must also assume the role of team lead and **"chief ego booster"**. Your job is to assure that your staff has the drive and incentive to get things done. To accomplish that, they need to know that you are there to support them with words of encouragement and a wherewithal of a person who understands mistakes because you have made them too. You need to show your staff that you are not happy with mistakes and that repeat offenders will face reprimand. However, at no time are you going to use their mistakes as a means of degrading them – or worse yet – public humiliation.

If you already have good control of your reactionary emotions, you could have skipped this section and moved on to the next chapter. Yet, I'd prefer that you take a quick inventory of who you are and how well you handle stressful situations. And, when you have a staff person who makes a very large mistake, can you to stand up and beg forgiveness from your management? How do you handle each of these ......

1. Discovering that an employee has destroyed original data for which there is no backup.
2. Finding out that you are out of balance by $541.89 – and have been for the last two months.
3. Watching as a portion of your department burns because a space heater was left on by accident.
4. Being lectured by a customer because one of your staff missed a deadline that directly affected their bottom line.
5. Receiving a warranted tongue lashing from your manager because three other departments worked all weekend to correct a problem caused by you and/or your staff.

And on, and on, and on.

Not good is it? All of a sudden early retirement looks really good – and you're only 26 years old.

Each of these is painful. But if your first reaction is to get your pound of flesh from your staff member, then you really missed the boat. You have to take the time to understand the problem as well as the cause. Once you have both of those, and a good idea of what the resolution should be, you can now direct your attention to the person or persons who caused the issue in the first place.

You now have the opportunity to be a hero instead of an ogre. You may not like what happened but if you do this the right way, you will really like what you create in the next 2-3 months. You will create a team of people who know what the bottom of the barrel looks like and they won't want to go back there again. They will not want to see another black mark on their personnel file and they won't want to see another "Labadie Look". (Apparently that is what my stare has been coined as being – when my eyes bug out and remain motionless as I attempt to shoot a laser look into the forehead of the person opposite me).

Keep your cool and keep your staff. Lose your cool and lose your job.

Fairly basic isn't it? The real story here is, once again, losing the respect of your staff. You can never regain something as valuable as respect. And, it should never be based on fear as that too has a "freshness date". Fear only lasts so long and then it becomes very old. The reaction of a person to threats and intimidation is either submission (on going poor performance) or retaliation (you definitely don't want to induce this reaction – it's not pretty).

So now is the time to perform all the assessments you need to assure that you are giving your team the best leadership you can. Solicit feedback and be sure you accept all feedback – good and bad – with the same interest and thanks. Once your employee walks out of your work area, you do not get a second chance at creating a new image of you as a manager.

Watch what you say, how you say it, when you say it and why you say it. If you are deliberate in your presentation, honest in voice tone and believable in demeanor, you will probably have little or no problem with your relationship with your staff. It is truly a gift that many people have and many more wish they had. It can be seen and recognized by senior management as a necessary tool for moving up the corporate ladder – especially if you maintain those qualities at times of stress.

Ever wonder how those people can stand in front of a gaggle of cameras and calmly respond to questions that require well thought out responses? They are definitely not camera shy! They are dripping of self confidence and are completely intimate with the subject matter. With enough patience and self control, you can perform at a similar level and give off the same aura. If your staff can see it, they can feel it. You don't have to tell them something they already know. Tell them something they didn't know – that, in your eyes, they are the ones to take on this new problem and resolve it.

Now, take a deep breath and read on!

Chapter 20: Emotion – how to handle it

"The closest I've gotten to reality is when my medication starts to wear off".

I have always had a problem relating a topic without placing at least six pounds of emotion into my correspondence. I had an executive VP who provided me with "emotion proofing". He would go through a proposed announcement and pull out the emotion leaving a flat statement that never suggested if I was in agreement with the statement or not. This guy was cool. You didn't know he was telling a joke until he got to the punch line and then you didn't know if you should laugh or not. If it wasn't a joke you'd look like a fool laughing while everyone else looked at the next guy to be axed during budget cuts. If you didn't laugh (assuming you thought it was funny) you had to find a way to keep from blowing a laugh out your nose – not pretty. It was very confusing.

So how do you manage your emotion - especially when you are the boss? It's not easy at all. I have found that it requires something that I don't have much of – *maturity*. It takes a good person to prepare a piece of correspondence that is presented factually and without bias. It takes even more to present it professionally.

I always instruct my staff to prepare a document (usually an e-mail) that could possess emotion and let it rest over night and read it again the next day after you have slept on the content. Usually, with a clear mind, you will see the emotion in your correspondence and re-write it or possibly discard it and drop the idea altogether. But every once in a while you follow through and really regret having sent the note while you are in the middle of an emotional frenzy. Not good!

So what can you do to help you handle your emotion or that of one of your staff members?

Let's look at emotion ....

e·mo·tion — (ĭ-mō′shən) *n.*
   1. A mental state that arises spontaneously rather than through conscious effort and is often accompanied by physiological changes; a feeling: *the emotions of joy, sorrow, reverence, hate, and love.*
   2. A state of mental agitation or disturbance: *spoke unsteadily in a voice that betrayed his emotion.*
   3. The part of the consciousness that involves feeling; sensibility: "The very essence of literature is the war between emotion and intellect" (Isaac Bashevis Singer).

I couldn't have said it better myself. "A war between emotion and intellect". Too often we are approached with problems that are 99% emotion and 1% problem content. Here are a few examples:

   • "If Bob doesn't stop stealing my ideas I'm going to leave!"
   • "Jennifer never asks me my opinion".
   • "Jeff is so focused on himself he rarely has time to ask his staff how they are".
   • "Who died and made Steve boss?"
   • "If a dime is worth 10 times more than a penny and twice as much as a nickel then why is it smaller than both?"

I apologize; I snuck the last one in because that one has been bothering me for years. But I hope you get my point. You will be approached daily – maybe even hourly – with questions like these and you must follow a very golden rule – "Don't laugh". Yes, no matter how silly or outright foolish they seem to a mature person, they are very serious statements made by your staff.

Think about it. Your office is close to their work area for a reason – so that you can communicate with each other. It is that fundamental proximity that will provide you with an office full of people when times are stressful and completely vacant when times are at their best. Enjoy the peaceful times because they are few and far between. You can be the best manager in the world and still have stressful times brought about by the economy, world news and events of the day.

These are the issues of the day for your staff so you have to treat them that way. Yes, you may have to suck your lips into your throat but at least you have a staff that trusts you enough to lay even the most trivial problems on you. Why? Well, mostly because you are the boss and they respect that. So, hand back that respect and hear them out. What initially appears to be a trivial problem could easily be one of far greater magnitude, once you have gotten down to the real reason for them dropping in on you.

And get ready for far worse:

- "My mother died last night and my father had a heart attack. I'm not sure what to do. Can you help me?"
- "I need time off for a hysterectomy. I've been advised that it is life threatening."
- "My life partner is leaving me and I'm not sure if I can handle the loss".
- "My son was picked up for possession last night and I need to go to the police station to provide bail for him".

Pretty sobering aren't they? And they are so very, very real. Each of them will bring a knot into your throat that you may not release for hours or days after they have walked out your door. And, just like any other management function, you need to finish your budget variance report before 5:00 and remember to pick up your dry cleaning after work, once you have finished with your follow up action plan for that person.

Welfare Balance

So how do you balance the company needs with those of your staff – and your peace of mind? Once again, it's not easy. But the bottom line is that they are **your** staff. That makes their needs every bit as important as your needs, when you are at work – maybe more. But you also have accountability with that responsibility which is to assure that you provide the best guidance with a 100% assurance that what you suggest is legal, morally correct and in line with corporate policy and guidelines. This is what will give you the sleepless nights and migraine headaches because you are never really sure that you are right. But the fact that you care enough to let it weigh on you means you have the concern of your staff ranked at the right spot. Just make sure you don't let the pendulum of stress swing too far over to one side or you too will become a victim.

The best way to manage these events is to remain focused, seek immediate answers and results and bring everything possible to closure as soon as possible. You cannot allow their emotion to activate yours. You must remain calm, focused and seriously brain active to listen to everything they say. You must then weigh it and provide a response that is not only in line with their statement or question but one that would make a room full of managers nod their heads in approval if they were listening in on the conversation. You do not have a choice, you have to be mature and honest in your response and have complete compassion for their condition and state of mind. I find the best way to respond to an employee is as if there was a Human Resources executive in the room with you. If you wouldn't feel right saying it in front of that person, chances are very good that you should not say it at all.

With that said, there is always the other end of the ultra extreme exchange with an employee:

- "If he says that again, I'm going to kill him".
- "If I don't get my divorce I'll be forced to run away with my family rather than let her win custody".
- "I don't have enough money to pay for a stamp. I have to find a second job or I'll lose everything".

These are classic examples of stress induced statements that demand your immediate attention. Not that the others don't have negative potential but these are very disturbing and need an immediate response with firm conviction. Granted, you may not have had enough training to spell the word "Psychology" but now you have to put your current knowledge and experience to task.

If you have access to an employee assistance program, use it! These people are the experts, not you. They know what to say, when to say it and how to truly help your staff members. If you are fortunate enough to have a company that supports this program, then you have landed a job with a company that accepts the overhead of providing the right kind of support for their staff.

There are PhD's out there who have put some wonderful books together that provide specific or general knowledge on how to handle stressful situations and the people who present them. I strongly urge you to get educated on how to manage them and yourself under all conditions.

Aggressive, distraught statements require immediate action. Too many people tend to sluff off these statements as emotional peaks with immediate emotional valleys. Then there is the all too well know expression of - **"going postal".** There is no room for ignorance or sarcasm at a time like this. Treat it like you see it. This has all the ear marks of a possible volatile situation. If you fear the person could get physical, get security involved as well as HR and your management. Your immediate action could possibly assist that person and turn around what could be a 5 o'clock newscast.

The best advice I can give you for this topic is "To thine own self be true". Be absolutely certain that what you do or say is something you would want to experience if the roles were reversed. Your employee deserves the very best treatment you can give – maybe even more.

Follow the Signs

So how do you know if you, a loved one, or someone who reports to you is suffering from burnout? There are several sources for the list of symptoms and early warning signs. However, one of the key signs is an obvious change in attitude and losing the drive to perform at the level that they have historically performed at, and been successful.

A few others are a feeling of hopelessness, frustrated and detachment. Granted, some of these are typical of an every day event that yields a failure. It is up to you to sort these out and attempt to determine if you have a problem that needs to be addressed. You can't allow yourself to go passive because you don't want to get involved or make a mistake. If you have a departmental reference source, use it quickly and let them approach the person for you. Take the guess work out of it and let an expert handle it from here.

Your job as manager is to look out for some of these signs – or clusters of them – and react to them immediately. I doubt anyone will take the time to thank you if you are right. But you can be certain that someone will approach with focused criticism if you are wrong. Your greatest asset – your employee – is depending on you at times like this. They won't want to talk about it but you will have to take your stance and be firmly supportive that you can and will help them through the process. It is more than a responsibility – it's an obligation.

One Last Surprise

I received an e-mail recently that was an attempt at correcting me because I stated that the way things were done five years ago were not necessarily the way they should be done today. The employee I directed it to then forwarded it to their manager and the manager responded. It surprised me because this person didn't normally offer a differing opinion from what anyone said. I decided that there was no reason to continue this as an e-mail exchange. I walked over to his office and very clearly stated as I entered "Do we have an issue here?" (I was holding a paper copy of his e-mail).

The person surprised me by dropping his head and stating that he was having a bad day and apologized for the way he crafted his e-mail to me. I know this man and he is one of the kindest people I have ever met and it had to have been an extremely stressful day for him to take the steps he did. Without hesitation I said "Don't apologize for standing up to an issue. It looked good on you!" You could read the surprise on his face.

I decided at that very moment that it wasn't important to be right – it was more important to let a very kind man know that I was proud of the way he stood up for his direct report.

His response was focused on the fact that it was presented aggressively and very matter of fact. I did not consider the feelings of the person being addressed. He, as a manger, was standing up for his employee – even if they were wrong. I thought the fact he stood up for his staff was commendable – even if he chose the wrong pretense. Frankly, I was proud of him because it was not familiar ground for him and although his timing sucked, his intentions didn't. So I praised him for his posture.

So do me a favor today. Surprise someone – especially someone you don't get along with very well – and find a way to tell them they are a better person today than they were yesterday. Don't search for the words as the best words quite often come naturally. You'll be doing more than making them feel better you'll be giving that person fodder for further personal growth and we can all use that. Besides, you'll be establishing yourself as someone who can see both sides of a situation and not just one. Not to mention the certainty they will have that you are having a breakdown and you will soon leave them with the keys to your car **and** your estate.

Chapter 21: PRESSURE!

"For years I thought Peer Pressure was when you tried to fit your entire basketball team into a Volkswagen".

Like it or not, you will be exposed to various forms of mental stress that may well determine your longevity as a manager. It may also determine how long you stay with Company "X". There are various demands that you will be confronted with that will have a lasting effect on you, your character and your ability to grow in your job. There is one thing certain, if you can't take the heat, stay out of the kitchen. You need to know what to expect so you can prepare yourself and create a plan for managing the stress that will be placed on you. If you don't, you will surely fail. If you don't know what to expect, plan for the worst and go from there. I always feel for those who expect the best. Those poor souls walk into a tree stump grinder face first and believe they'll come out of it without a scratch. The only thing you can do as a friend or relative is hope they remembered you in their will.

Pressure takes many forms. There is office politics, peer pressure, customer demand and job stress. Each has a reason for existence and each has a means of being managed. What you have to learn is how to recognize the signs and react with conviction.

Office Politics

Office politics is probably the most difficult area to manage. You have absolutely no control over most of it, you have to be an expert to successfully play and the only benefit of playing is moving up a ladder that has very few rungs – especially for those who have a weak footing.

Unless you are seeking a role as a very senior executive or a senior manager who will be exposed to the world of politics, I strongly suggest you avoid it like the plague – when at all possible. It places a huge demand on your energy level. It has far greater risks associated to failure than anything else you manage or control. It requires an expert who lives by the process and, once started, you cannot randomly stop. It is outside your control the second you assume you have it under control.

Granted, there are times you have to play the game because it is expected of you. That does not mean you have to like it, want to continue doing it or feel compelled to justify it to yourself. Playing the game means that you have to know who is in charge and who is best at manipulating people, numbers and procedures. If they are all rolled up into one person – watch that person because he or she will go a very long way. What you have to determine is how far you are willing to go with that person.

I'm not very good at that process. I care too much for people to manipulate them. I know enough about numbers to know when someone is hiding facts and if I can't trust them, I sure don't want to work with or for them. And, I have far too much respect for proper procedure to force myself to jump steps knowing that if I don't pay the price, someone else will. So, now that you know I'm a sap, you can easily manipulate me.

There is no doubt in my mind that the greatest people in politics are the greatest manipulators. That is why I will never be famous or note worthy - although I do make a great Shrimp Alfredo. Your decisions have to be entirely wrapped around who you are and what you are prepared to be – to be successful. If you can do it without sacrificing your grandmother or your first born, then you will probably do very well and still be able to sleep at night. You still have to have a natural taste for blood – not ruthless – but ready to execute when required, to be successful. "The greater the prize, the more the risk". Just make sure to look over your shoulder every once in a while so you know where you came from.

Now be careful here. Some office politics is normal and quite acceptable. For example, if you know your CFO likes seeing presentations that reflect minimum capital spend and short term lease alternatives you need to cater to his or her preferences when ever you are looking for project approval. If that person is managing the company purse strings, you need to think their way. If your CEO is holding you and your department to a specific head count but will approve temporary or contractor support to complete a project and you have a tight deadline, then it behooves you to make certain your proposal has temporary labor in there. If outsourcing is the word of the day, use it to the advantage of your team and your company.

If you find yourself asking "Why should I cater to their preferences?" I have to say that you need to support your team by getting the job done and if getting it done means catering to the personal preferences of your executive, then that is exactly what you need to do. It is imperative that you understand you are a first time manager and until you get the attention of your senior management, your differing opinion (unless you are extremely profound and amazingly capable of leading small armies) is best held to yourself.

It is very important that you understand when to go with the flow versus turning around and taking on the entire organization. For the sake of your team, you are expected to "work smart". You should be looking at alternatives to reach your objectives because each time you do, you come closer to the next step of visibility – being a known achiever. If management sees you as the person to "get the job done", they will prefer that you lead versus someone else.

Once again, don't confuse what you just read with kissing anyone's posterior. Working smart means that you consider all of the areas that will affect your ability to be successful. But don't confuse being successful with rising to the top. Success is measured first by your ability to do your job correctly, then by how expertly you do it and finally by how well you represent your company, your team and their performance. Working alone, misleading your management and misrepresenting your team will eventually lead to isolation, mistrust and lack of credibility – ergo unemployed. Yes, there are always exceptions but I'd rather bet on something that has a 99% success rating then something that has a 1% opportunity for success.

It's your call!

Peer Pressure

This can be a powerful tool or the end of your career. Peer pressure is the pressure applied by a work associate who reports to your manager or one of the people who also reports to your manager's peers. You know them more as your organizational equal.

These are the people who are potentially eligible for the job you report to. So what could possibly happen that would be negative? Well, look around. Of all the people you have as a peer who would you not want as a boss? Now you know what there is to fear. I had that happen. A person who at best can be called a very intelligent person who just happened to be a hypocrite - became my boss. When he eliminated my position he tossed my severance package on my desk and walked out saying "have a nice day". I expect it gave him great pleasure to do that because I had absolutely no respect for him and didn't hold back my opinion.

But I wasn't smart enough to realize that there was a very strong possibility that I would some day be reporting to him because senior management loved him. Why? They loved him because he got the job done. Even though the majority of what he did was unethical or inhumane. So I treated him like the person he was. It was definitely a mistake on my part. I didn't have to treat him any differently than anyone else. I didn't have to respect him but I didn't have to disrespect him.

I learned from that as well. It's easy to put someone whom you dislike for any given reason into a category of "Jerk". It takes a very well-put-together (I don't believe that to be a legitimate word but most everyone knows what I am attempting to say) person to work with that person and remain successful. I obviously wasn't mature enough to find a way to work through the rough parts of the road with this person. It cost me my job while it elevated his very large ego.

There is a very positive side to peer pressure. ***Competition.*** That is why I loved the student work term program. It allowed my department to bring in fresh young talented students who loved to ask "why" – much of it to the chagrin of the older more technical personnel who hated change. Soon after starting with us, the students learned as much as they needed to in order to be productive. That's when the real return on investment came about. They could now produce at the same speed – if not faster than – the old timer. And it was at this time that they started **CHANGING** the way things were being done.

Yes, that four letter word –plus 2 – that makes the heart accelerate and sweat glands work overtime. The one word that will make every employee consider retirement and the same word that can turn an also-ran company into a leading competitor – ***Change***. As soon as it starts happening it is like a snowball rolling down a steep snow covered slope. It eventually overtakes everything in its path and soon everyone is changing – or leaving.

Now ***THAT*** is peer pressure. It is when one person tries something new that reduces manufacturing time by 15% or reduces the weight of a car part by 22% without reducing the strength of the part itself. It is a program that runs 76% faster or a fabric that is 90% stronger. All of these are results of change and peer pressure. Joe finds a way of providing a 3D image of a heart X-ray and Brenda figures out a way to send it electronically to Fred's PC. Gupta then takes that image and projects it on to a 70 inch screen at a medical convention and the viewing audience sees the surgical result of a quadruple bypass.

Peer pressure is good. The only time it is bad is when one of the peers cannot compete and finds a way of posing as a competitor by stealing ideas, lying about ownership and hiding underhanded processes. That is the risk of having a person collapse under peer pressure and the manager could not see the symptoms.

I love peer pressure because it stabilizes the mood of a team. It allows people to honorably compete to bring the other person up a notch while each person on the team seeks a new, more competitive level. It turns workers into improvisers and rockets the intellectual into futuristic discoverers. It turns resentment into enthusiasm and resistance into creative drive. I have seen far more lost souls turn into happy productive people than I have arrogant mediocre performers become unemployed. It is a delight to see people stretch their minds and stand proud over the results. It is a work of art created by a team and admired by a management body.

Customer Demand

This is an easy one for everyone and yet sometimes impossible for many – servicing customer demand. Frankly, the customer isn't always right and it takes a very good manager to know when to correct the product and when to correct the customer.

A customer walks in and is very irate because their dry cleaning was soiled even after it was cleaned. They paid for it and when they got home and yanked off that annoying plastic, their silk blouse was still showing the perspiration stain it had when they dropped it off. They insist on talking with the manager. You win – they want to talk with you.

You have an array of options available to you but only one will work for this customer – offer to clean the garment at no charge and, in addition, give them two coupons for free suit cleanings. And, you offer a very sincere apology. It is clearly evident that you failed to provide the service level expected. The blouse has that wonderful stapled tag indicating it had been cleaned. You have a team of people who are supposed to inspect the clothing before releasing it. Even if the stain is impossible to get out, you missed the quality check so now you have to pay the price – twice.

Now, if the customer decides to bring your family heritage into the discussion, you have the permission of society to remind them that this was a mistake that can be corrected and that your family heritage should not be part of the conversation. If they insist on creating a scene you should execute the last stand which is to repeat the offer, apologize again for the mistake and advise the customer that you will personally call them with the results of the next cleaning. Or, you can refund them their money with the promise that they not come back to your store. The problem here is – who really won? It wasn't you even though you felt good waving goodbye with your $4.75 in their hand. So, how important is it to be right?

I was watching one of my sons play soccer when a boy from the other team came up to my son and intentionally tripped him from behind to get the ball. Like any absorbed parent I stood up beckoned the only available intellectual property I could retrieve and screamed out to the opponent's coach "Is that what you teach your players?" The coach stopped in his tracks and replied in an amazingly calm voice. "You don't really mean that do you?" I was uncontrollably mute. He was dead right and to top it off, I knew him as a fellow employee and also knew he was a heck of a fine person.

So what possessed me to say that? I sat back down and realized I was extremely small. I allowed a simple game to get control of me and blurted out words of anger that I would have never said if I were disappointed with him in a business capacity. I suddenly realized he was a much larger and better man than me and I admired him for his ability to maintain his calm while those around him could not.

I learned from that and I hope it makes enough sense to you that you can learn from it as well. There we were at both ends of the spectrum. My end was labeled "Village idiot" and his was labeled "Classic example of composure". Someday I want to grow up to be just like him.

PRESSURE!

I can remember my boss, VP of Information Technology, witnessing a severe problem I was managing and once it was resolved, he stated "How the heck do you do that?" – to which I blindly replied "Do what?".

He had a strong voice that rose as his frustration or surprise increased. "You handled that like it was an every day occurrence". I replied that it was an every day occurrence. He shook his head, smiled and went to his next meeting.

Am I a rock under pressure? Sometimes I am but I lose it just like everyone else when the demands are greater than the resources I have available to me or the frustrations are too many and the rewards too few. Working in IT as I do, there are problems every day and you have to look at every problem as an opportunity to correct an issue that should never have happened. You saw my four steps to resolve every problem earlier in this document. Maybe I should have added a first compulsory question – "who's in charge?"

In order for you to lead the way to resolution, you have to have full control of the resources. It doesn't mean you have the right to issue orders or set people straight. In most cases, the people working the problem know how to fix the problem. What I can provide is support, guidance, positive acknowledgement and some fairly good logic, when needed. For example, a major circuit fails and over 40% of our regional offices are down and cannot connect to our mainframe. There is absolutely nothing you can do to fix the problem in the next three minutes so use that time to get your thoughts together. Plan your action relative to what needs to be done to contain the problem, recognize common symptoms, define it and identify the personnel who can fix it once and fix it fast.

A network problem requires a smart vendor to view the network from their window while your smart technicians and engineers look at it from their vantage point. The two together – assuming one is reliable enough to be truthful with the other – should be able to isolate the problem and determine the time to repair of the failed device. As manager, my job is to echo their findings back to them and assure they are following procedure. I attempt to keep them honest by avoiding assumption and pointing it out when ever it occurs. By performing those few tasks consistently and predictably, my team can quickly zero into the problem area and resolve the issue. If I lose my cool or show signs of being out of control I send negative vibes to my staff that makes them question their direction and elongates the resolution time. They doubt their ability to be successful and begin to question their findings and the foundation of their logic. They become an un-guided missile.

 If leadership is questionable, those being led have no foundation for success.

Accepting the truth

I firmly believe that I can handle most everything thrown at me in my line of work. But ask me to give CPR to someone involved in a violent automobile accident and I toss my cookies and pass out. To me, that is the real world of pressure – trying to save lives. My hat is off to those who place their lives on the line every day and think nothing of .....

- scampering up a 10 story ladder to save someone they don't even know from burning to death
- diving into freezing cold water to save a small child from drowning
- deftly manipulating a scalpel to remove a cancerous growth without touching a vital organ
- flying into hurricane force winds to pluck a crew from their sinking ship
- charging into a building to prevent a gunman from hurting a group of innocent people

So what pressure can I possibly experience that is greater than death defying? None! And I'm very pleased to say that is the correct answer – for me.

However, there are many, many people who react to pressure as if their life was on the line and that is truly unfortunate. They make very poor decisions and seldom enjoy their job or their staff.

They desperately need to back out of that frame of mind and into one of customer support and personal satisfaction. It is way beyond survival. It is preventing you from reaching an early grave with all the physical byproducts of stress. Weight loss, gaunt facial lines, overnight bags under the eyes, gray skin pigments and much more are some of the results of stress. These are people in their late 40's and they blend in like chameleons at a retirement home.

So why does this happen? There are probably far more answers than I can possibly dream up but I can personally vouch for a couple of them ....

1. Caring too much and
2. Letting those with little or no influence make you believe they can negatively affect your life.

Caring too much is when you invest all of your time into your job, your staff and your relationship with the "users". I often wondered how a collection of investors or owners were called "users" in the IT world. I am certain it was initiated with a perception that the people "used" the computer output. But as my career elongated with time, I realized it was actually looking at the negative side of a line of business where you occasionally run across those who "use" you, your position, your resources and your life energy.

When ever there is a production problem, there is always going to be someone who will unequivocally declare you as the problem and walk away feeling that they have done society a great favor by doing so. These people are usually the ones who knock over a beverage with their elbow and look at you as to why you allowed that to happen. Sadly, I have to admit, they are sometimes correct and you will have to accept the fact that the truth will periodically come from the mouth of those with the mental capacity of a garbage can – and you will have to live with it. Some of you take it far too personally and attempt to prove to that person that they are wrong and here are the reasons as to why. Do you think they really care? They now have you on the defensive – right where they want you. You are now morally obliged to cater to their every whim by reacting and over-reacting to anything they say or do that you perceive as an aggressive act to deface you or your team. You, and your team, just lost.

Take early retirement while you can still form words without salivating on your shirt.

I would never tell you to discount anyone, let alone the person who is probably footing your bill. But if you want to maintain sanity and support a positive environment for your staff, you have to find a way to educate those people. Or you will have to find a way to document their requirement in the form of a service level agreement – one that you can measure and meet. Then, every time they complain, point to the document that proves you are meeting or exceeding expectations, and move on. It assures you will reach old age, unless you have a habit of forgetting important things and love sky diving. The best part is that your staff reached old age too – because you managed their environment the same way you managed your problems.

The second problem is when you let those with no influence drive you to drink. Let me give you an example. A manager with a desire to quickly elevate finds that your reports are not correct. Instead of bringing it to your attention, he walks the problem in to your boss who then brings you in to listen to his version of the right way of providing service to a "paying customer". You then take it upon yourself to correct the problem and state that it will not happen again. It doesn't, but this person shows up with another problem and suggests it is a continuation of poor service.

This is where you make a decision. Do you pull together all the resources available to prove them wrong? Or do you seek out a voodoo specialist so you can drive long needles into an ugly doll while drinking the blood of chicken's severed head? Or do you reiterate what you did last time and leave out the fact that it will never happen again.

Take door number three. The first has no return on investment because you are using a wrecking ball to hammer a finishing nail into the wall to hang a picture. The second is downright nasty. The third corrected a statement made when you were trying to stress that your team is qualified – but they are not perfect so don't make commitments that you know you can't keep. Apologize for the problem and ask them to come back with any other issues. You already know he or she will be coming back so don't fuel the fire with promises they even know you can't keep.

The key here is to **know your enema**. No, that is not a spelling error. I repeat. Know the person who provides you with the most pain and discomfort. Don't try to give them any better service than any of your other customers unless you are on the verge of losing their contract. At that moment the risk and the reward are very clear. But even then, sometimes you have to tell the customer that it was fun working with them but their demands are greater than what you can provide. They are therefore fully entitled to go to someone else for their business. It sends a very clear message to them that you have reached the peak of your current efficiency and that you cannot meet their expectations. You have then officially kissed off a customer. You need to know and prove that your service level is at the top of the vendor heap or what you just initiated is a mass exodus.

I must advise you that you had better have the support of your boss before you draw either conclusion. Assuming you did that, you may have decided that this person was stepping far outside the realm of pointing out a service problem. He or she was either seeking your head or the glory of exposing a horrible wrong that was nothing more than a data entry error from his staff. Don't let a service problem turn into a battle of egos. The key is to always come out on top with a happy customer and a continued contract.

Those were only two very small examples of how a person can destroy everything they have worked for because of over commitment or unsubstantiated demand. Yet, if you are to be a successful manager, you will have to learn a great deal about the people you work with and work for. By knowing more about what makes them tick you can be a better provider and a far more satisfied human being. That alone, allows your staff to go home at the end of a long day and know they contributed towards something important. And they will have far more energy to come in Monday morning if their manager is a person they feel is one who represents them professionally. They also need to feel that he or she is someone who stands behind them to allow them to bask in the glory of success and, when required, will stand in front of them to protect them from the vile customers that are out there.

There's your goal – now set your standards.

Chapter 22 – Read, Listen and Observe!

"I find I learn more when I listen with my eyes".

I cannot think of words that better express the "manager's creed" in being able "to humanely manage, mentor and provide the best example to your staff of what being a manager is all about". Your persona is partially created by anyone you have looked up to and who has an air about them that emits self-confidence, honor and credibility. Who are these heroes? That's easy – they are your parents, your best friend's parents, your pastor, parish priest or rabbi, your favorite teacher, a military figure, government official, a movie star, a world leader, a hall of fame athlete, a previous manager. All of these people have a place in the special section of your mind reserved for people who helped mould you into the person you are today.

Finally, we have something that the word "accountability" can lovingly point to with the intention of passing on beatitudes instead of the "it's your fault" index finger wag. Far too often accountability is used in its negative context and not the positive side where "Bob is accountable for the profits of this organization and he's doing a great job too".

Like it or not, you acquired that feeling of respect because of what you read, heard or observed. From it, you drew your own conclusions because you used that person as a reference point to fill a void in your life. You deduced, either consciously or unconsciously, that this person was a good person because of your current or newly acquired beliefs. That person just provided you with a sense of direction and because of him or her, you are about to do something you have never done before. This could easily be the turning point of your career or life. And, thanks to this person, you will enter into a new segment in your life that may end up being the best decision you could have made. A decision like getting your masters or doctorate, traveling to a foreign land or seeking a career in space travel, could be the reason for you discovering a cure for a devastating disease.

Now, that is what I call exciting! Imagine, you could be the reason why someone you are mentoring discovers the cure for cancer, a vehicle that permits time travel, a source of perpetual energy or cure for balding that doesn't require any form of paint spray. Sorry, ever since my hairline went from receding to full retreat I have been sensitive to people who are insensitive to people who go bald. Maybe that's why I am always impressed with people who see me as a person with a knowledge base and not a sixty year old bald spot between them and a punch bowl.

I have always felt sorry for those with no sense of sharing inside their character. These are the people who hold their knowledge close to the vest and refuse to document or hand over the "knowledge rights" to their personal database of educated discoveries. They have a huge fear that what they just gave to you will mark them as obsolete and eliminate their beloved role in life. This is usually not a position held by a parent or community leader but rather a business partner or peer – someone who perceives you to be a competitor, not a youthful ball of learning pores that absorbs knowledge because it is so darned much fun to learn.

You, my friend, are different. You don't care if your staff learns your job because you can continue to grow, just as they are, and assume more responsibility in either the same line of work or a different arena. That is because you are not paranoid and you do not fear the unknown unless it is in a foreign restaurant staring at a crusty green substance on a plate and everyone around you is saying "eat it, it's good for you". You are in fact mature and ready to prove it by helping someone else meet or exceed your knowledge base. But first, you have to be in a position to educate and instruct. Surprisingly enough, it might be that same junior technician who will be teaching you by one of the oldest methods known – listening!

Listening

Sorry, come again? I couldn't hear that, do you mind repeating it please? **What?** Each of these is a request to have someone repeat something "because you are interested in what they have to say". Some of the nicest people I have met are incapable of hearing. They don't have a hearing loss or even a reduction in hearing. They chose not to hear. They evaluate something (or someone) in advance and if it does not meet their standards, they cannot hear it. They can't see, feel or smell it either. It just doesn't exist. Haven't you ever known someone like that? Think back to when you were very young – less than 10 years old – and you were introduced to someone at your church who acknowledged you as a child and then moved on to the next person. They had that artificial smile and the nauseating hand gesture where they pat you on the top of your head. You immediately didn't like that person. They had absolutely no interest in you because you offered them nothing they wanted. It is still happening today. That person could be one of your peers, your boss or your boss's boss. It could be a member of your executive, your mail person or AA. It could be a manager from another department – one that does not need your expertise. But they definitely exist.

Can you recall when someone came to you looking for information and the second they realized that you did not have the information they needed, they ignore you and moved on to the next person. You tried to get their attention to refer them to someone else but they suddenly became deaf. Even if you raised your voice they kept moving away from you.

Is it possible that you are like that? I hope not - especially to your staff. They deserve, even on your worst day, your full attention because they have plenty to say. Stop and take the time to really listen to what they have to say to you. And, if you don't understand, make them repeat it so you feel the impact of the full statement. Then mull it over in your mind before you respond. Make certain that you fully understand what it is they are saying and the damage you could cause if you answer it incorrectly. Whether it was related to how your company manages the 401 K or what their bonus might be this year, they deserve a full and accurate answer to their question. And it must also be in line with what they asked and not a slightly modified response so that it suits your needs at the time.

Each time you are approached with a question or an idea from someone on your staff, place that person in your shoes and psychologically reverse your roles. Make them feel your perspective. But most of all, listen to the question so you can determine the depth of your response. Make certain they do most of the talking and keep your answers short and precise.

The key is to make certain they understand that they are being heard. You are listening to every word and you are encouraging them to expound and explain. You are giving them something that, in their eyes has huge value – YOUR TIME!

The real question here is "How important is it to be heard"?

I do have a hearing impairment. When I was around seven, I was playing cowboys with my two best friends. One of them snuck up on me and fired his air gun into my left ear and to this day I depend heavily on hearing from my right side. That's my excuse and I'm sticking to it. However, it wasn't until I got married that I realized how much I block out what is being said so I can focus on what I wanted to hear. Nancy has told me many times that I don't listen to her. I kept brushing her off stating that she didn't speak up enough or that I just wasn't paying attention. Eventually I had to learn how to listen to her because she reached a point of frustration with me that was going to end with me wearing an electric carving knife in my nose if I didn't change. I changed!

It was true. If I didn't feel that what she was saying was going to be important, I'd block out what she said because "she was just making a statement that yielded no interest for me". My goodness I really was a male chauvinist jerk. So if I was doing that to her, was I doing it to my staff, my sons, my friends? Undoubtedly, I was. So I had to start on a quest to start listening to what people had to say so I could better relate to them. What I didn't realize was that I was about to experience a series of learning experiences that would make me a better person –and much, much wiser.

I began by taking myself away from something that I felt was more interesting – like television. I was really brain dead when I watched TV. I would get so wrapped up in what I was watching that anyone in the room could stand up and announce they were committing suicide and I'd either ignore their statement or provide a monotone response of "That's nice". That had to stop – and quickly. I believe I've made better progress but I now know that if I'm watching something I'm really enjoying, there are new tools out there to help me – like "pause" on a DVD. There is also the "Mute" on the remote control for the TV. Or, if it is really important – I now know how to hit the "OFF" button. That one takes a great deal of conviction to press – especially if John Madden is providing play-by-play as to why the wide receiver was not in position to catch the ball. It's a start and the person who knows you very well also knows what it took for you to do that, so they are appreciative of what you did and will get to the point even faster because of that.

I also started taking far better notes of what people were saying at meetings. I historically took notes of things I wanted to do as a result of the meeting but seldom wrote down what people were saying. That one change allowed me to reflect back on what was said so I could better relate to what they wanted – and not what I thought they wanted.

The point here is to show an interest in what people are saying and make a commitment to listen to them. It is the very least you can do. Besides, you expect them to listen to you, so extend yourself into their world and let them know you really care. ***You do, don't you?***

I'm not saying I saved my marriage or that I am a far better husband. I know that I still have a long way to go before I can classify myself as mediocre. But I spend fewer nights on the sofa fighting for a larger sleeping area than the dog. That alone is worth it.

The key to every successful relationship is that both parties have to want to listen to the other person. Being heard is more than a positive elixir for the mind. It is the vehicle for common bonding between two or more people and a source of vast knowledge. Besides, saying something out loud is quite often the foundation for discovery. It assists in establishing credibility of theory and soon evolves into a documented solution.

WOW! That was exciting!

Observe

I was in New York City many moons ago with my manager, Dave. As I walked the streets for the first time, I looked way, way up and saw something I had only ever seen on television – the Empire State building. What excitement I felt – even at the age of 30 – to be inches from the building that the entire world focused on for so long as the world's tallest structure and a symbol of American ingenuity. I had to get to the top and see it for myself. Besides, I had to see if King Kong left any marks on the building when he lost his grip before falling.

Dave had a voracious appetite for many things but most of all it was learning something new and seeing something for the first time. He was game! So we began our trek up several different elevators and stairs until we got to the top and saw a stunning view of New York. As I wandered the roof top available to me, Dave placed his twenty five cents into a telescope and soon afterwards called me over to it. With only a look that Dave could give when he had something hidden in his mind that was soon to unfold, he called me over to the telescope with only a few words. "Here look at this and tell me what you see".

With the hesitation of young woman opening a small box that just might contain and engagement ring, I brought the telescope up to my eyes. It displayed a full view of the top floors of .... the Empire State Building. With that, Dave broke out into a belly laugh that I will never forget because it was definitely one on me. Oh, and by the way, as it turned out, we were on top of the Rockefeller Center. Close, but no cigar.

Assumption can be a horrible waste of time or a tremendous learning experience. One can be devastating and the other so very rich and rewarding. It all starts with observation, then deduction. The twist towards correct identification is based on how well you observe and the strength of your conclusions. One mistake and you have only misguided assumptions.

As a manager, you are expected to observe. You have been doing it all your life and especially after you started your first job. You observed what was exciting and new to you. You watched your boss to see how she managed her work load. You watched the department AA because he or she knew the ins and outs of general mail, express delivery, the fax machine and the photocopier. You watched your peers – in particular old man Purdy, because he had the best sales numbers and got the biggest bonus checks every month. You observed and soaked up everything that was important to you so that you could improve your knowledge base, increase your value and elevate your responsibilities.

How about your staff?

Look closely at what your people do every day. Their actions are the basis of their conclusions. Watch the way they communicate.

Body language is a powerful statement. Do they gather in one area to work with one another or do they communicate by e-mail when only a few feet from one another? Do they spend time as a small group at lunch or at a break? Do they stay after work just to talk about their accomplishments – or failures – before calling it a day? Or do they spread out like a shotgun blast as soon as the clock strikes 5:00?

You probably cannot change the way they interact with one another as that was happening long before you came along. But you can change the way they work together during the day. If they honestly feel like peers, they will work like peers. What you learn from observation, may well allow you to plant a seed of camaraderie that could grow into a strong self-supporting structure of unity. You may also discover why some parts of your team squeak and that will allow you to develop a plan on how to get them well oiled again.

I'm not saying they will name their first born after you but if you can provide the direction to making them a better team, put your pillow down and rest because you have made some serious progress.

Read

I have already mentioned that if you want to get serious about improving yourself, you need to read far and beyond this text. Being a solid manager means you need to be strong in your specific field. It also means that you need to be extremely effective as a leader. That is why you need to seek out texts and whitepapers on your field of passion like Architecture, Finance, Manufacturing, etc. and absorb them. You need to be able to read and practice what you read. Use it as a source of conversational fodder with your staff and see what happens from there. This is where ideas are born.

The best way to get to know your staff is through relational conversation. I have found that the information I was exposed to in high school was the best source of material for relating to anyone and everyone. History, Geography, Social Studies and even foreign languages are an excellent source of breaking the ice with your staff and getting them to open up to you.

Have you ever noticed how easy it is to converse with people if you can relate to their native land? Even if they are from up state New York or from the mid West or the deep South, all you have to know is a little bit about where they are from and you can talk a considerable length of time about just that topic. Now, try it with your staff. I guarantee you that the path to winning them over as allies to your cause starts with you relating better to them as individuals.

I can think of numerous times that I was able to almost immediately win over a new person by greeting them in their foreign language – even if they didn't speak the language. I met my Hispanic manager in Chicago for the first time many years ago and by greeting him with "Ola!" I got the response "Sorry, I don't speak a word of Spanish – my parents wanted me to speak English". That spoke volumes to me about him, his parents, his beliefs and why I wanted this young man reporting to me. He was immediately my first choice for succession planning. I promoted him two months later.

How can you get closer to your staff? Read about them. It doesn't matter if they are young and you are older, read about their likes and dislikes. Whether it is books, movies, games or favorite TV shows, you need to have a common point of reference in order to get them to relate to you, their jobs and the company.

Speaking of which, read about the company. The more you know about your employer, the better you can understand why they have the policies they do. You can better relate to the benefits provided and explain them to your staff. Read the articles – positive and negative – so you get a more diverse view of how your company is viewed by those outside the organization. Get a solid perspective of what your customers think and why. Read about the corporate objectives and why they have those objectives. This is the very core of why you have performance reviews – so you can compare the goals and objectives of your staff to those of the organization.

Read and then share your knowledge with your staff. It's not showing off – it is fact sharing. Anything you can give them will make them more valuable to you and the company.

Closing the gap

You have read as much as you can and you are searching for more. You have, and will continue to observe your staff and listen to everything they tell you. You are indeed informed and proactively involved with your staff and their future. It's your future too. Everything that you can pass on to your team will allow them to better emulate the type of manager that you are – open, considerate and extremely capable.

Being effective in your role means that you are interacting with your staff and providing enough constructive tension to get the job done. You are not looking for new friends but rather close allies. Keep yourself from getting too close and preventing you from being direct when you need to be that way.

Your new information acquired from reading listening & observing will be extremely accurate data that will allow you to reach your objectives with people armed and ready for a challenge. You must also use that data for your employee reviews. Because of the information you have about each of your staff, you can now provide a true 360 degree view of who they are and what can be done to improve their position with the company and build a stronger future for them. You now have reference data for personal growth. Take that and add the tools available to you through training and education and watch them grow.

You done real good.

Chapter 23: Retrospect!

"Why is it people are searching for the fourth dimension when they can't even see the third one"?

I have to tell you, the older I get the more I have available to me as **retrospective reference**. It's a shame I couldn't have found this in a bottle and inhaled it or swallowed it to have immediate reference to previous history. I could have made far better decisions. You are in the same boat. You are starting into a new world of challenges that you are reasonably prepared to handle but you are nearly void of reference source. Or are you?

What about your parents and your favorite teacher in high school or your all time favorite instructor in college? How about your last boss? Every one of those people has some history in working with people, helping them become better people and getting them over job related and personnel humps. They have the retrospective view that you, as yet, do not have. Use them as your personal resources. I assure you, they will not complain because you are allowing them to use their intellectual property so you can amass yours.

The sad part about getting older is what you lose – like immediate recall of names, places and events. I thought it was terrible to lose my hair when I was a teenager but it is far worse to lose your memory and forget your grandchild's name. It's humiliating!

So, if you've got it – use it! Teach someone a little of your past today. Pick up a book and read it so you can compare their thinking to yours. Then form your own conclusion – and then pass it on to someone who needs to know. Open yourself to someone who needs help and see what you get back. Soak up the resources available to you through your associates, friends and family who have a serious age edge on you. If you can spare the time to ask them a question, I assure you, they can spare the time to respond.

I hope that this book has given you a few more tools that will help see you through at least one day of problem management. My vain attempt at dumping what little knowledge I have into these few pages has already been rewarding for me in that I was able to spend less time in front of the television and more time in front of a monitor trying to figure out why I insist on spelling "fro" instead of "for". God, I hate keyboards! I will be so much happier when I can talk into a device and it can accurately spell what I mispronounce.

I do wish you the very best in your career choice. I wouldn't trade all my years of management for anything. Now, a few of them I would gladly give away at no charge but overall, it has been exciting, rewarding and sometimes downright invigorating. There is nothing better than watching someone take the ball and run faster and further than you ever could. I ask that you put everything you can into supporting your staff because someday you may be reporting to the dumb, skinny little kid with the big glasses and that really weird smile. What a DORK!

Final Chapter: The HIT List – Don't go home without it!

"The only difference between the beginning and the end of a book is the attitude you have when you are reading it".

There are two appropriate times to present this list to your boss – the day you are offered the job and accept your manager role or your first day on the job and you want to hit the ground running. Personally, I prefer handing it to my manager the day I accept the job offer. That gives him or her a couple weeks to prepare the information. And, what he or she gives me (based on what I asked for) on my first day of work speaks volumes about the kind of manager he or she will be *for me*.

Here's your checklist or "initial information bible" …………..

1. Org chart of your new team showing head count and open positions
2. Org chart of my boss's team and the person to whom he reports and the teams reporting to my peers.
3. Executive org chart: Your manager's peers and his or her manager.
4. Upper Management org chart of key support areas / customers - Operations

5. List of your employees with their birth date (excluding year) and company anniversary date
6. List of each employee's anniversary (start) dates
7. What are the anniversary years of recognition from your company (1, 5, 10, 15, 20, etc.)
8. Budget – current and historical – separated by each area of responsibility
9. Building floor plan of each facility supported by your department
10. List of projects for your team – by department – with owner & due dates
11. List of projects being supported by this team – participants – and the project owner with due dates.
12. List of projects that you will be associated with for various reasons.
13. Summary of all departmental statistics and reports provided by each manager. Historical summary of the efficiency of each statistic – are we improving?
14. List of SLA's supported by each department
15. Problem management summary – by month
16. Monthly/Weekly reports to be produced by the data center team.
17. List of hardware and software supported – including network layout
18. Departmental awards – who won the award(s) and as recent as when?
19. Training & education budget – how well is it being used and is it adequate? Who is currently scheduled for training?
20. Succession planning – who is doing it – who isn't?
21. Strategic Planning – who is and who isn't participating?
22. Problems – where are they and who has any ideas on correcting them?
23. Is there an RCA (Root Cause Analysis) process? Who manages it? Who reports it?
24. What internal measurements are being kept? Anything not reported to the customer? Are they accurate?

25. Do they keep quality metrics? If they do, what are they and who is the one collecting the data? Who records it?
26. Salary review – when was the last one taken and what changes have been made in last two years.
27. Job Descriptions – for each role.
28. Departmental Documentation – how good is it and who is responsible for it?
29. Your department Standards & Procedures – what is used to create these and how good are they? Embryonic? Solid? Somewhere in the middle?
30. Who performs the QA work? Who performs the QC work?
31. Management Policy. Procedures and Practices Manual.
32. HR resources available to management – Employee Help Line, etc.
33. Holiday Schedule
34. Round up your employee personnel files – and read them
35. Employee vacation summary (vacation entitlement for all staff members)
36. Expense items: cell phone, ISP Internet access, etc.
37. Company credit card – how do you handle travel expense charges and reimbursement? Business cards – who coordinates? What title?
38. List of your departmental assets, current depreciation and book value
39. List of key department heads (Finance, Human Resources, etc.) and their phone numbers
40. List of current vendors and your key sales and support contacts
41. Delegated authority list – what is yours and do any of your staff have signing authority and for what amounts?
42. Hit list from your boss with key areas to address in a specific time frame.
43. List of your customers and their contact numbers
44. List of Corporate and departmental goals and objectives (yours too)

45. Request a list of items and areas to address. Then, create your own personal list of items and areas to address. Compare your differences and be prepared to sit with your manager and discuss the differences.
46. Either ask for a planning tool or get one yourself. Then, plan your learning process for the next 3 months based on all of the above – review and adjust it daily.
47. Outline your strategic plan for the next year – your previous plan should feed into it. Then, review after 30 days and personally commit to it in writing

Feel free to add to this list. Your line of work will easily add to the items you need to reference when you first walk in the door. People in manufacturing roles have similar but different requirements from those in Finance. Managers in retail have a very different role than those in government positions.

Keep in mind that this is the platform for your learning in the next 3 months and the subsequent planning base for the balance of the next year. It will represent the very foundation for your questions, the types of answers you get and the assumptions you will draw from your interviews.

Now, you are ready to kick some serious butt! You are armed and extremely dangerous. The question is – to whom will you be more dangerous – you, your staff, your managers, your peers or the problems that each of them has that you can potentially solve?

Have fun!!!

About the Author

Ray Labadie is a forty-plus year member of Information Technology (IT). He has been fortunate enough to have occupied every job role in IT from operator to database application developer to auditor and on to international strategic planner. For over thirty years, he has managed people. His travel has taken him through North America and a frequent flyer to France, Germany and England.

His love of IT began as a unit record operator for a public utility in Chatham Ontario Canada in 1965. While shuffling hundreds of thousand of punched cards in Unit Record every day, he was amazed at the way the whole process worked. And, one day while picking up a tray of cards and sliding them into place on the sorter it finally hit him as to why he had to sort the cards backwards in order to get them into numerical or alphabetic sequence. From there, it was a matter of literally drinking from a fire hose.

Thanks to the support and patience of his favorite manager, Jack Morrison, he chose systems programming where he spent a few years coding in Assembler and then programming in COBOL. It was here that he started his management career.

Ray developed and installed his first major system with this same public utility before leaving to work in a technical and pre-sales role with Sperry-Univac. Ray soon received a job offer from one of his accounts to become their technical analyst. From there he went on to assume ownership of a technical team and soon after that - the data center – his first true love. Then, thanks to open minds of his management, Ray was spending a great deal of time in Europe and the United States helping different data center managers resize or re-shape their data centers. He designed, built, staffed and managed data centers in Canada, Auburn Hills Michigan and Atlanta Georgia. He also built three Network Operations Centers in the Atlanta area where he assumed management of the network operations center for the world wide corporate network. His area of responsibility was North, South and Central America.

After 20 years, Ray left this large international company to assume a series of senior management positions in two Dot Com companies, a credit and collection company and a Call Center. Ray joined the staff of Security First Network Bank. Once again, an acquisition took place but this time the bank asked Ray to assume the directorship of the infrastructure group of a bank in North Carolina. Today, Ray works for yet another bank in North Carolina doing what he loves most – managing their data centers. By the way, he's rebuilding their production and Disaster Recovery data centers.

Mr. Labadie taught COBOL, Assembler and Computer Operations at St. Clair College of Applied Arts in Chatham Ontario. For seven years he worked with his students to create the prototype of the first commercial version of the portable computer room. He also gave several presentations to colleges, local governing bodies and IT affiliate organizations in Ontario and Michigan.

Ray has an absolute love of the work term student concept. Because of that, he has attempted to initiate the creation of a training program for students from local colleges and universities. The process allows the students to rotate between his or her college and a sponsoring company so they can acquire a degree and have as much as two years of work experience when graduating – a foundation for nearly a guaranteed job.

Next to writing, Ray loves to teach. Whether it is through his job or at a local college, he enjoys the opportunity to educate someone on how to improve themselves as well as the output of their work day. He has always found that he learns far more from the hungry minds of a student than he does through casual or project related reading. Ray also found that no matter what he taught, the student always asked questions that he could not answer and thus coined his first acceptable response **"I don't know, but I'll find out"**. He sees all growth as the result of improving your output – no matter what the activity. One of his favorite expressions is *"How important is it for you to be right – and how important is it for you to do the right thing?"*

This book was actually the idea of one of Ray's direct reports, Karen, who felt he should put his teachings to paper so that many can enjoy his sense of humor and all that life has taught him. That is exactly what he has done in completing this book.

Ray began his first day on the job as Director of Infrastructure for a North Carolina based bank by greeting his staff with "**Hi, I'm your new manager**"!

Reference Credits

American Heritage Dictionary (www.Dictionary.com) provided the definition of "emotion":

American Psychological Association (APA):
emotion. (n.d.). *The American Heritage® Dictionary of the English Language, Fourth Edition.* Retrieved May 29, 2007, from Dictionary. com website: http://dictionary.reference.com/browse/emotion

Chicago Manual Style (CMS):
emotion. Dictionary.com. *The American Heritage® Dictionary of the English Language, Fourth Edition.* Houghton Mifflin Company, 2004. http://dictionary.reference.com/browse/emotion (accessed: May 29, 2007).

Modern Language Association (MLA):
"emotion." *The American Heritage® Dictionary of the English Language, Fourth Edition.* Houghton Mifflin Company, 2004. 29 May. 2007. <Dictionary.com http://dictionary.reference.com/browse/emotion>.

www.ingramcontent.com/pod-product-compliance
Lightning Source LLC
Chambersburg PA
CBHW031835170526
45157CB00001B/314